D1234291

FIFTY-FIVE FATHERS

DISCARD

FIFTY-FIVE FATHERS

The Story of the Constitutional Convention

SELMA R. WILLIAMS

Illustrated by Robert Frankenberg

DODD, MEAD & COMPANY

NEW YORK

Copyright © 1970 by Selma R. Williams

All rights reserved

No part of this book may be reproduced in any form
without permission in writing from the publisher

ISBN 0-396-06228-8

Library of Congress Catalog Card Number: 72-127170
Printed in the United States of America
by The Cornwall Press, Inc., Cornwall, N. Y.

To Burt, Pam and Wendy

75-10861
CENTRAL ARKANSAS LIBRARY SYSTEM
BOOKMOBILE DEPARTMENT
700 LOUISIANA
LITTLE ROCK, ARKANSAS

AUTHOR'S PREFACE

There is a conspicuous lack of material on the Constitutional Convention, written for young teen-agers. As a former American history teacher and mother of two teen-agers, I have long been dismayed when attempting to find books on this exciting—and compulsory-in-the-curriculum—subject for supplemental reading or book reports.

An attempt to make James Madison's notes on the Convention of 1787 immediate and understandable to students provided the inspiration and source for much of *Fifty-Five Fathers*. Descriptions of delegates were based on the diary of Major William Pierce, Convention delegate from Georgia. Additional anecdotes and narrative passages were culled from a lifetime of research and reading about the Constitution both as student and as teacher.

Each day at the Convention James Madison, seated by special permission at the front of the hall, took notes of everything spoken in debate—including his own words. Immediately following each session, according to the preface he wrote to these notes, he spent several hours clarifying his transcript and, in the few instances where available, comparing advance texts of speeches with words actually spoken.

Madison reported all speeches, even his own, in the third person. His eighteenth-century language is sometimes quite formal and full of unfamiliar words and phrases. In addition, his abbreviations are occasionally difficult to decipher and his spelling is inconsistent. Some very long speeches go on for several pages of closely printed copy, and are both complicated and repetitious. Other speeches confuse the issue by being restated frequently and cropping up in the middle of a debate on a totally different subject.

Despite these difficulties, Madison's notes remain the single best primary source on the Constitutional Convention. Therefore, in an effort to convey to the reader the excitement of conflict and compromise and the interplay of gigantic intellects—but with special attention to preserving the flavor of the original—dialogue and debate have been freely adapted.

Special thanks are due to Emily Page, librarian, Diamond Junior High School, Lexington, Massachusetts; to Margery Howard, reference librarian, Cary Memorial Library, Lexington; to George Carr, teacher of American history, Diamond Junior High School, Lexington; and to two teen-age advisers, Matthew and Craig Goodman, of Washington, D.C., all of whom took time from busy schedules to read the entire manuscript and to offer valuable ideas. Thanks are also due to William Whipple, my editor at Dodd, Mead & Company, who offered many helpful suggestions.

Any errors are of course unintentional and completely the responsibility of the author.

CONTENTS

PROLOGUE

PROLOGUE

Summer came very early that year. By mid-May the heat was intense. But in Philadelphia, the nation's largest city and its capital in 1787, at least one building kept its windows tightly sealed. Secrecy was more important than fresh air.

Inside the Pennsylvania State House fifty-five of the nation's most powerful and talented men were beginning to gather. Their presence was no secret—only their proceedings. Some had well-known names: George Washington, Benjamin Franklin, James Madison, Alexander Hamilton. Others were easily recognizable as they went from meeting place to living quarters, for they were surrounded by servants and dressed in the fashion of the times.

Like a uniform of aristocracy, they all wore buckles of silver fastened just below the knee on their breeches, and stockings of imported silk. Their waistcoats were long and their coats were open almost down to their knees. Several wore wigs that were carefully powdered and beribboned.

Most of the delegates could claim vast experience in the

art of politics, having served as governors, members of Congress, or state legislators. More than half were lawyers, with the rest describing themselves as physicians, educators, merchants, and planters. Benjamin Franklin referred to himself simply as "philosopher."

An urgent call sent to all thirteen states had brought them to Philadelphia. The country was facing the worst crises of its eleven-year existence. Independence, for which they had fought a revolution, had replaced tyranny with chaos and confusion—plus the threat of foreign intervention.

Frightened by their experience under the British, the thirteen former colonies had carefully avoided setting up a strong central government in their own constitution, the Articles of Confederation. Instead, they had set themselves up as an alliance of thirteen almost-independent nations. They followed this scheme even during the Revolutionary War, when states had supplied men and money to the central government on a purely voluntary basis.

Rapid population growth alone was just one of the factors making this plan of government too casual and ineffective. There were two and a half million inhabitants in 1776 at the time of the Declaration of Independence, and four million now in 1787, just eleven years later. Certain problems such as foreign policy and commerce—between states or with other nations—could be settled only by the individual states. Moreover, if the national government was to be effective, it needed the power to levy taxes.

The list of troubles seemed endless. Spain was conducting guerrilla warfare along the border between Florida and Georgia and was prohibiting United States occupation of the east bank of the Mississippi River, land ceded by Britain in the Treaty of 1783. Britain herself was nibbling away at provisions of the Treaty, beginning with a refusal to abandon fur-trading posts along Lake Champlain in New York, and in Detroit.

Absolutely alarming was the recent experience of Massachusetts, whose appeals for help in putting down Shays' Rebellion had to be ignored by a weak central government with no men or arms at its disposal. The rebellion involved eleven hundred farmers who were angered by Massachusetts' refusal to issue paper money so that they could pay their debts. The farmers, led by Daniel Shays, a captain in the Revolutionary War, used the methods proven so effective against the British. They prevented the courts from sitting, so that no judgments for debts could be issued, and they attempted—unsuccessfully—to get arms by raiding the Springfield arsenal. Only after almost five months of near anarchy did the state militia finally defeat the rebellion.

Seven months previously, just before the Shays' Rebellion, Virginia had tried to call together all the states at Annapolis, Maryland, to discuss common problems. When only five states showed up, the delegates adjourned with a recommendation to the Congress of the Confederation—in which all states were represented—that a new convention be called. Congress kept putting off the issuance of such a call until February 21, seventeen days after the final quashing of the Shays' Rebellion, which had by then thoroughly aroused the entire country.

Representatives had begun arriving in Philadelphia by twos and threes on May 14, the date set for formal opening of the Constitutional Convention. However, some states refused to recognize the existence of a crisis and failed to respond immediately, while many of those willing to answer the call were delayed by bad weather and poor transportation.

Even before the actual meetings started, Philadelphia added to the tense air of mystery by going to great lengths to protect the privacy of its guests and to keep them from being disturbed in any way. Guards were posted outside the doors. And from the very beginning the city assigned workmen to shovel loose dirt over the street in front of the convention hall in an effort to quiet the clatter of passing wagons and carriages.

These special considerations were particularly welcome to the delegates, beset by conflicting emotions. They were thrilled at the chance to mold history, yet frightened by the responsibility involved. Secrecy might be possible during the Convention, but afterward Philadelphia, the nation and, in fact, the whole world would judge the outcome.

THE CONVENTION

CHAPTER ONE

"WE'VE DONE nothing but sit around wasting time the last eleven days!"

Everyone was startled into absolute silence. The speaker, Robert Morris of Philadelphia, had the reputation of rarely opening his mouth in public. Now, however, the words tumbled out.

"Representatives have finally arrived from seven of the thirteen states. I suggest that our Convention organize immediately."

"Hear! Hear!", shouted the delegates.

Encouraged by this response, Morris continued: "I move that our great hero George Washington be elected presiding officer."

Former Governor John Rutledge of South Carolina seconded the motion. A unanimous vote and loud applause followed. George Washington rose and bowed. At the age of fifty-five he was a big man—six feet two inches tall, two hundred pounds, size thirteen shoes. Almost immediately Morris and Rutledge appeared at his side to accompany him to the front of the hall in the awesome Pennsylvania State House where the Declaration of Independence had been signed.

Washington had difficulty making himself heard because of badly fitting wooden teeth. But his first words showed he had not changed much since assuming command of the Continental Army under the elm tree on the common at Cambridge, Massachusetts, twelve years ago: "Please give me your forgiveness in advance for any unintentional mistakes I may make. I am quite inexperienced in these matters."

Then he warned gently: "I know that you will all understand that we must have absolute secrecy of debate. Nothing spoken or written in this convention or in any committee can be revealed to anyone—not even your family—until we have adjourned permanently. Gossip or misunderstanding can easily ruin all the hard work we shall have to do this summer."

At this point Washington's young friend from Virginia, James Madison, rose to make a request in a voice so quiet that those sitting two rows back had to strain to hear him. "May I have permission to sit in the front of the hall with my back to you, Mr. President, so that I may take daily notes of all proceedings? We ought to have a complete record of this Convention for future generations—to be published after adjournment, of course."

At thirty-six Madison was a small, frail man—five feet four inches tall, one hundred pounds—with the reputation of being an intellectual giant. Before Washington could answer, Madison added, "I wish also to be allowed to participate in debate."

Without hesitation Washington granted permission for
both requests. Then he turned to sharp-nosed George
Wythe of Virginia, sixty-year-old professor of law, who
had been patiently waiting for recognition. Before saying
a word, Wythe approached Washington's desk to hand
him a neatly written paper. Then he returned to his own

place to request, "Mr. President, will you please read for the Convention's approval the rules of procedure which the Virginia delegation has drawn up?"

Rising to the importance of the Convention, Washington read with pursed lips and the famous look that froze men into silence:

"(1) All delegates are expected to rise when addressing the President.

"(2) No one may walk in front of a speaking delegate.

"(3) Delegates are not to read books, magazines, newspapers, or pamphlets at their seats during debate."

Then pausing to dart a meaningful glace at Delaware, which despite its tiny size and population had one of the largest delegations at the Convention, Washington continued sternly:

"(4) Each state may have as many delegates as it wishes, but each state will be allowed only one vote. All motions are to be passed or rejected by a simple majority of states present and voting."

Hearing no objection to these rules, the President continued: "Every member will find at his seat a copy of the fifteen resolutions drawn up by the Virginia delegation to correct and enlarge the Articles of Confederation. I propose holding them over for debate till next week when perhaps additional states will be represented. Today being Friday, please plan to study the entire document carefully over the weekend.

"It is already three o'clock. Will someone please move that we adjourn to give ourselves time for private consideration and informal discussions?"

There was almost a stampede as several delegates eagerly

rose to their feet to comply with Washington's request. They had been in the hall since morning. The meeting had opened formally around noon, and they had been too excited to take time for lunch. They were tired and hungry.

As they left the hall they congratulated themselves on an excellent job of organizing the Convention. They assured each other that Washington as presiding officer was sure to transfer his own great prestige to the proceedings. And the rules they had adopted meant firm but fair treatment for every point of view.

Of course, many could also be heard muttering about Virginia's domination of the meeting. Robert Morris, it appeared, had been wrong to denounce *all* delegates for sitting around and doing nothing the past eleven days.

CHAPTER TWO

AFTER A WEEKEND combining serious discussion with gay social activities—a dance for delegates and their wives, a dinner in Benjamin Franklin's new dining room—the delegates reassembled Monday morning at eleven o'clock sharp.

The sight that greeted their eyes stunned some of the out-of-town delegates, although Philadelphians took it quite for granted. Benjamin Franklin was entering the hall on a lavishly decorated golden sedan chair, carried by four husky convicts. Over the weekend he had heard that the Convention was about to get down to serious business and decided that despite the pains of gout and advanced old age— he was now eighty-one-years-old—he must be present.

He had imported the sedan chair from Paris. It suited his needs perfectly, transporting him from place to place without unnecessary jiggling. Privately he chuckled with his friends over the special pleasure he got from this chair, invented for the comfort of spoiled aristocracy: "Imagine using such a contraption for my convenience. I've spent my whole life fighting the very idea of an aristocracy!"

Three more states had now sent representatives to join the seven states already in Philadelphia. But only Maryland and New Hampshire were still expected. Rhode Island, tiniest of the thirteen states, had denounced the very idea of a Convention, making it quite clear that she would send no one.

Rhode Island strongly supported the present Confederation, adopting as her own motto Thomas Paine's words, "That government is best which governs least." At suggestions that her name ought to be changed to *Rogue* Island or that she deserved to be dropped from the Union and have her lands divided between Connecticut and Massachusetts, she simply snorted.

New York had almost joined Rhode Island, for she feared that the Convention would abolish states' rights. But her governor, George Clinton, had no particular admiration for the present government under the Congress of the Confederation, which had consistently refused to honor New York's claims to Vermont territory.

Slyly—and with the backing of many powerful New Yorkers—Governor Clinton concocted a plan whereby he named three delegates to the Convention: Alexander Hamilton, whose views on the need for a strong central government had given him a not-to-be-ignored national reputation, and John Lansing and Robert Yates, Albany lawyers who belonged to the governor's states' rights party. To ensure that New York would always favor states' rights and that Hamilton's views would never prevail, the delegation was instructed to vote only when at least two members were present and participating.

Several Convention members were quietly discussing Rhode Island's sullen attitude and New York's distinct lack of enthusiasm when Washington pounded his gavel to call the meeting to order. He immediately nodded to the tall, distinguished-looking governor of Virginia, thirty-four-year-old Edmund Randolph.

Randolph's voice rose with fervor as he said: "There is too much democracy in this country. The people must be curbed. Somehow we muddled through the Revolutionary War with the Congress of the Confederation. But it is now the twenty-eighth of May in the year 1787, six years since the last guns were fired in that war, and four years since we signed the peace treaty.

"We are in a terrible predicament. It has proved impossible so far to change or improve the Articles of Confederation because we can never get all thirteen states to agree. We need a totally new constitution with a different form of government. Unless our government can be made stable, we are going to suffer worse tyranny than we did under the British."

A murmur of surprise swept through the hall as many delegates asked, "But what will become of our states?"

Undisturbed, Randolph continued his denunciation of the Articles of Confederation after reminding the Convention that he was a state governor who stood to lose power under a different constitution. "There are too many situations in which the states are weak and incompetent. The present Congress is not worthy of our great new country. We need a strong national legislature—so strong that it can throw out any state law which conflicts with the new constitution.

"We can never be a nation as long as each state is allowed to pursue its own foreign policy, or impose customs duties on goods from other states as though they were foreign nations instead of part of the same country. Nine states even have their own navies. Worse still, half the states have begun printing the words 'dollar' or 'ten dollars' or even 'one hundred dollars' on ordinary pieces of stationery which they then dare to pass off as money.

"There isn't even a supreme court to decide quarrels between states. Therefore, on behalf of the Virginia delegation, I move that a national government be established, consisting of a supreme legislature, executive, and judiciary.

17

Once we have agreed on this general scheme, we can work out the details."

At this, forty-three-year-old Pierce Butler, probably South Carolina's wealthiest resident, jumped to his feet. An Irishman by birth who was now an American citizen, he had no love for England. He reminded everyone that it was exactly the strong government of England that had brought about the Revolution. "Is there no other way besides throwing out the Articles of Confederation and adopting an altogether new form of government? Our government declared its independence only eleven years ago. Are we really old enough, experienced enough, to try a form of government never used anywhere in the history of the world?"

Scanning the room, Butler noted the absence of several leaders of the Revolution. "Thomas Jefferson, author of the noble Declaration of Independence, uses as his excuse the fact that he is presently our ambassador to France. Likewise, John Adams is our ambassador to the Court of St. James in London.

"But there is no question that others stayed away to express strong disapproval. Patrick Henry—you all recall his moving speech, ending 'Give me liberty or give me death' —said of this Convention that he 'smelt a rat' and refused to come. Richard Henry Lee, who proposed the resolution in the Second Continental Congress which led directly to the Declaration of Independence, declined to be a delegate from Virginia. Samuel Adams of Tea Party fame in Boston and Thomas Paine, author of the famous Revolutionary pamphlet *Common Sense*, spoke out against the whole idea and were not even invited.

"In letters and in private conversation these men have made a strong case on behalf of keeping the Articles of Confederation. The Articles, they point out, provided the government which won the war against powerful England —and obtained twice the territory of the Thirteen Colonies through the Treaty of Paris which ended that war."

Butler continued: "These leaders do not trust the delegates of this Convention, who are wealthy aristocrats, to pay attention to the needs and rights of all the people. No one is here to represent the small farmers, city workers, debtors, frontiersmen—the bulk of our population. Perhaps amending the Articles would be enough—instead of discarding them completely for a new and untried constitution."

The debate continued all week. Some argued the necessity for a strong national government. Others defended the Articles of Confederation as carrying out the spirit of the Declaration of Independence. Exchanges were often bitter.

By the end of the week, disturbed at this dissension, Governor Randolph decided to proceed more carefully in an effort to win support for a strong national government from all delegates. As chief spokesman for Virginia he delivered a three-hour speech to assure the Convention that the proposed legislature would not replace the legislatures of individual states. Then he suggested an immediate vote on his motion to replace the Articles of Confederation with a strong national government, separated into legislative, executive, and judicial branches.

Several delegates asked recognition to voice approval. Unbelievably, the first speaker was none other than the same Pierce Butler who had deplored attempts to discard the Articles of Confederation. "I have over the past week studied carefully Governor Randolph's scheme. I wish to announce that I have changed my mind and now favor establishing a national government. The idea of separating this government into three equal branches—legislative, executive, and judicial—is ingenious and will certainly guarantee that there can be no tyranny.

Then Charles Pinckney, thirty-year-old delegate from South Carolina, rose to plead: "Consider this plan seriously. We must not lose history's first opportunity to establish a government of peace, harmony, happiness, and liberty."

James Madison, interrupting his note-taking at the front of the room, added: "We are now going to decide forever the fate of government for the benefit of the people."

The final speaker was the strangely named Gouverneur Morris of Philadelphia. The two Morrises at the Convention—Robert and Gouverneur—were not related and were alike only in the name Morris. Gouverneur was born into wealth (which may have accounted for his aristocratically French name), exuberant, still somewhat of a playboy at thirty-five despite having lost a leg while racing a horse. He loved being the center of attention as he spoke in public—which he did often and brilliantly.

He concluded: "The whole human race will be affected by the proceedings of this Convention. Those of you from New England and the South who have doubts can take your choice—a strong central government now or a tyrant-king before twenty more years have passed."

In the end the delegates voted to scrap the Articles of Confederation for a Constitution with a strong national government. Only Connecticut opposed the motion. New York's two delegates who were present could not agree. Alexander Hamilton favored the motion, while Robert Yates opposed it, so New York's vote was canceled out and could not be counted.

Nathaniel Gorham, eloquent state judge from Massachusetts, now rose to suggest convening at ten in the morning on Monday. "Longer hours and harder work are necessary. We have much to do. We have so far accomplished very little."

Without waiting for recognition, Virgina's Governor Randolph snapped in response: "You may be right that we need extra hours. But how can you say that we have accomplished little? We practically voted a second revolution when we agreed to change and strengthen our government."

"Gentlemen, you are tired," Washington said soothingly. "You all deserve great praise. Now let us adjourn for the weekend."

CHAPTER THREE

BENJAMIN FRANKLIN had the happy talent of turning an ordinary occasion into an elegant event. An expert on conversation as well as on good food, he gave magnificent dinner parties.

Personally, though, he preferred talking to eating. In his old age he had difficulty standing on his feet while speaking. But seated at his dining table, he could hardly be kept quiet. He fascinated his guests for hours on end with stories of his life as American ambassador to Paris during the Revolutionary War, or of his many careers, any one of which would have been enough for an ordinary man—inventor, publisher, printer, politician, and diplomat.

Knowing his reputation as a storyteller and fearing for the secrecy of Convention proceedings, several delegates conspired at the very beginning never to leave him alone during public or social appearances outside Independence Hall at the State House. And so it happened often that on the verge of revealing even an unimportant detail, Dr. Franklin found himself being diverted to talk instead about the weather (raining or unbearably hot), the latest fashions (outrageous), or the new buildings in Philadelphia (beautiful).

The delegates did not even want the public to know their procedures. They kept secret their vote turning themselves into a Committee of the Whole to debate the Virginia Plan.

Every morning for almost three weeks George Washington would walk in his soldier-like manner to the desk in the front of the hall and gavel the Convention into order. Then each time he would carefully explain that he was giving up the Convention presidency to the elected chairman of the Committee of the Whole, Nathaniel Gorham of Massachusetts. Within a matter of minutes from the time he had arrived at the front of the room, Washington would bow formally to Gorham and walk stiffly to his seat in the hall.

The Committee of the Whole sometimes struck the Convention as almost comical even though it was highly practical. The members of the Committee were all the very same men who were delegates to the Convention. But now they were able to talk to one another as they might in someone's living room. They did not have to follow the usual procedure of waiting for recognition by the chairman each time they had something to say. The only limitation on speaking out was a polite desire not to interrupt someone else.

Without the rigamarole of formal motions and seconding speeches, they could vote off-the-record for or against various suggestions and ideas. Best of all, there were no formalities if they later changed their minds and decided to use what they had earlier thrown out.

Chairman Gorham, using all his eloquence and judicial experience, remained calm even when denunciations flew and tempers flared over the apparent lack of faith in democracy. Roger Sherman, a shoemaker's son who was now a state judge from Connecticut, argued strongly that the people should have no part in their own government: "They are too stupid and can be easily misled."

Sherman's speech did not arouse much argument because it was dull and made in a difficult-to-understand Yankee accent. The delegates simply ignored him. And this despite his claim to special respect. Sherman, Robert Morris of Pennsylvania, and Elbridge Gerry of Massachusetts were after all the only three delegates who had signed both of the country's basic documents, the Declaration of Independence and the Articles of Confederation.

Nor did Elbridge Gerry himself present much of a threat to democracy with his stammering, slow delivery. "Every evil in the country today can be traced to the fact that we have too much democracy. The people do not want virtue, but are the dupes of pretended patriots."

Fortunately, one of the people's strongest defenders turned out to be at the same time one of the country's best speakers. At the age of sixty-two, white-haired George Mason was old in years but young in ideas. His five-thousand-acre plantation and great wealth gave little hint of his liberal outlook. He had been the author of the much praised Virginia Declaration of Rights, included in that state's constitution to protect the people against tyranny.

As any good debater, he started by making a concession

24

to his opponents: "I admit that we have been too democratic, that the government established by the Articles of Confederation has not been strong enough to maintain law and order."

But then he continued: "I fear that we may go to the other extreme if we are not careful. We must protect the rights of every class of people. I often wonder at the indifference of the upper classes. Just on the grounds of humanity and their own selfish interests, they ought to realize that they may be wealthy today but in poverty tomorrow. Therefore, even if they care only about themselves and their own families, they ought to favor a system that would provide as carefully for the rights and happiness of the lowest classes as for the highest classes of citizens."

Edmund Randolph waited politely, but with some hint of exasperation, for Colonel Mason to finish and take his seat again. To Governor Randolph, any discussion not focusing directly on his delegation's carefully drawn Virginia Plan was a frivolous waste of time. Forcing himself to sound diplomatic, he said in his musical voice that made even ordinary language sound like poetry: "As an examination of democracy this whole discussion on the extent of democracy has been most interesting. But, please, let us confine ourselves to the practical problems of government. In other words, let us debate the specific details of setting up an actual government for the United States."

CHAPTER FOUR

SOMETIMES IT SEEMED like the end of the world that summer of 1787 in Independence Hall, Philadelphia. The delegates themselves added to the almost unbearable confusion by their unexpected departures. Before the Convention was ten days old, George Wythe, a strong member of the Virginia delegation, was forced to leave permanently. His already invaluable contribution as chairman of the Committee on Convention Rules and his encyclopedic knowledge of law had led many to expect to lean heavily on him. But now his wife was desperately ill and needed him at home.

Nor did the weather offer much encouragement. Almost at the beginning George Washington had to send a servant on an eight-day round trip to Mount Vernon to get his rainwear and several umbrellas. Everyone was getting daily soakings—except on the days when the weather turned sunny and inhumanly hot.

There was an almost impossible amount of work to be done. Every new decision set loose a hundred problems to be discussed and solved. So, despite the weather, the delegates decided to meet six days a week, including Saturdays.

The delegates were conscientious and took time to listen carefully to all proposals. Thus they were polite in hearing Benjamin Franklin's suggestion that the legislature should consist of only one house. They readily acknowledged that Pennsylvania had been able to get along with just one legislative branch. But they made the point that the Congress of the Confederation had failed with a similar setup. Therefore they overwhelmingly rejected the proposal.

Like others not at the Convention, Thomas Jefferson was at a loss to understand the near-unanimous feelings on this subject, when he received Madison's reports after adjournment. Years later, on his return from France, he was invited to coffee by George Washington. Smilingly, the President watched as Jefferson poured some of his hot coffee into the saucer: "I knew you would do that. Now, explain why."

"To cool it, of course," the younger man answered.

"Well, then, you should be able to understand why the Convention thought two branches of the legislature were necessary—to cool passions in much the same way."

There were no cool passions when it came to debating the matter of representation in the legislature. Following precise instructions from her state government, tiny Delaware went so far as to threaten to withdraw completely from the Convention when she learned that the large states were demanding representation based on population—the more people, the more representatives. As chairman of the Congressional committee that had framed the Articles of Confederation just ten years ago, John Dickinson of Delaware continued to believe strongly that only a few changes would be necessary to correct any defects in the present setup of a league of thirteen almost independent nations. Now he exploded. "Rule by a foreign power would be preferable to domination by large states."

It took tremendous efforts behind the scenes to convince Delaware to remain. Always the peacemaker—and the Convention's most frequent speaker—Gouverneur Morris of Pennsylvania asserted: "There would be real concern if the

Convention were to lose the valuable assistance of Delaware. And if any state withdrew from the Convention, the country—indeed, the whole world—would take it as proof that our new nation is a complete failure."

Then to save Delaware further embarrassment and to give her time to reconsider, the delegates agreed to discuss other parts of the Virginia Plan. They postponed until later this key question of representation.

Meanwhile, Governor Edmund Randolph of Virginia took it upon himself to dine every evening with a different group of delegates. He would always steer the conversation to Virgina's plan for representation. Sometimes pounding the table for emphasis, he would say: "Population must determine representation in the new legislature. Virginia has exactly sixteen times the population of Delaware, and will no doubt be expected to contribute much more money to the national government. Therefore, even if it means angering Delaware again, it is only common sense that Virginia should have exactly sixteen times as many representatives. The worst mistake we made in drawing up the Articles of Confederation was to give each state equal representation regardless of size and wealth."

As Governor Randolph had intended, word of his arguments finally reached the Delaware delegation. They met privately to adopt their own strategy, and they decided that the best way to defend the interests of their small state was constant attendance and participation at the Convention.

When serious debate on the legistature began in the Committee of the Whole, Governor Randolph again assumed his familiar role of spokesman for the Virginia Plan. "The legislature is, of course, the heart of any national govern-ment—as we came to realize when the British Parliament ruled us. And like the British we should have a lower house or House of Commons, elected by freemen, and an upper house like the House of Lords and representing our own aristocracy."

Here Randolph paused for effect, then continued slowly as though underlining every word. "And above all we must keep strongly in mind that population must determine rep-resentation in the new legislature."

Predictably, the delegates from Delaware and several other small states broke into an uproar of disapproval. Ob-viously, private dinner conversations with Randolph had not succeeded in changing their minds. Chairman Gorham was forced to pound his gavel a full three minutes to restore order in the Committee of the Whole.

James Madison at the front of the room observed quitely: "There are really two issues here. One is how to determine the actual number of representatives each state will have in the legislature. The other is how to choose these represent-atives. Should they be chosen by all the people or be ap-pointed by a small group in each state?

"In other words, what should be the role of the people in their own government? Should they take part in their own government by choosing their own representatives? Or should they allow a few aristocrats to choose these representatives?

"It seems to me," Madison went on in his scholarly man-ner, "that the issue of how to choose representatives applies equally to all states. But the same cannot be said for the question of the specific number of representatives for each state. I suggest, therefore, that we discuss first the problem of choosing representatives, but leave the size of each state's delegation till later."

There was general agreement. The delegates could not do anything about the miserable weather, but at least this arrangement seemed to be a way to make a difficult debate somewhat easier.

Some delegates amused themselves by predicting what a man would say as soon as he rose from his seat. This was not too difficult in the case of Connecticut's Judge Roger Sherman. Everyone knew his views opposing election by the people, even though he himself was no aristocrat.

Nor was anyone surprised when Virginia's aristocratic George Mason, a strong believer in democracy, came to the people's defense, arguing strongly for election of at least the larger branch of the legislature by the people.

But everyone was at first puzzled when James Madison's rival for the title of "Convention intellectual," James Wilson, rose to his feet. This distinguished Philadelphia lawyer, who was both friend and admirer of Benjamin Franklin, showed the delegates a large picture of a pyramid. They soon understood his intention when he pointed to different areas of the picture, saying: "We must raise our federal pyramid to great heights and therefore should give it as broad a base as possible. No government can last long without the confidence of the people."

Taking the opposite point of view, the brilliant Alexander Hamilton of New York, a persuasive speaker—and, at the age of thirty, one of the youngest delegates—rose to denounce democracy. He concluded, "The people do not have the intelligence to determine what is right."

And Elbridge Gerry, that wealthy Massachusetts merchant, voiced his usual arguments—in his usual stammering manner. He stressed that he strongly disliked the idea of election by the people. "Our situation is completely different from that of Great Britain. Therefore, a House of Commons cannot be expected to work well here. Just by way of example, several of our states have very bad legislatures, even though they were elected by the people."

He was joined by aristocratic Pierce Butler of South Carolina who agreed, observing that election by the people was most impractical.

Then James Madison spoke again. As always, his speech carried a great deal of weight, for it was based on a life-long study of men and their governments since the beginning of written history. "If we are to have free government, one branch of the national legislature absolutely must be elected by the people. If the people's wishes are not taken into consideration, there will be no sympathy between them and their rulers. The fabric of government can only be stable and durable if it rests on the solid foundation of the people themselves."

It turned out that despite what seemed like a large number of disapproving speeches, most of the delegates favored election of the first branch of the national legislature by the people. Six states voted "aye"—Massachusetts, New York, Pennsylvania, Virginia, North Carolina, and Georgia. Connecticut and Delaware turned out to be divided, so their vote did not count. And two of the small states, New Jersey and South Carolina, voted "no."

After the meeting several delegates teased the Georgia representatives about voting with the large states. One

Georgian retorted huffily: "We may be small in population, but we have tremendous land area. And someday we will undoubtedly be the country's largest state when our claim is recognized to all the land from the Atlantic Ocean to the Mississippi River."

The answer, dripping with sarcasm, came right back: "You won't be the country's largest state when that happens. You'll be the world's largest country!"

CHAPTER FIVE

THE DELEGATES remained convinced that a second legislative branch was necessary to keep the first branch from going off on a frolic of its own. Later, using grander language, scholars expressed the same idea in the words, "Two branches of Congress are needed, each to serve as a check and balance for the other." But still unsolved was the problem of how to choose members of this second branch.

One victory had gone to those who favored election by the people for members of the first branch of the legislature. Now everyone except James Madison of Virginia and James Wilson of Pennsylvania, the two intellectuals, agreed that there had to be some sort of victory for the losers. Otherwise they might feel that since no attention was being paid to their ideas and feelings they might as well pack up and go home.

And so the delegates made the first of many compromises, thereby setting the pattern that on all difficult questions each side would have to give in a little for the final success of the Convention. They quickly agreed that the state legislatures would choose members of the second branch of the national legislature. This was a clear victory for those favoring government by aristocracy.

Now Maryland's delegates finally appeared in Independence Hall, and with their long-delayed arrival, the Convention considered itself representative of the whole country. Eleven of the thirteen states were present and New Hampshire was rumored to be in the process of raising funds for the long trip to Philadelphia.

Taking this latest arrival as an encouraging omen, the delegates moved on to consider the power to tax—that all-important power which had brought about many revolutions, including their own. But again tempers flared. Everyone agreed on giving the national legislature the right to tax. The hotly debated question was where tax legislation should originate. Should both branches at the same time propose tax laws? Should whichever branch had the idea first be allowed to propose this kind of legislation? Or should the first branch alone have this power?

James Madison feared jealousy might arise between the two branches if one had an important power denied to the other.

Hugh Williamson, a North Carolina physician who loved to debate even though he was a poor speaker, questioned whether money legislation always had to originate in one branch rather than the other. However, if this were proven the case, he strongly advised giving this privilege to the second branch where such legislation was bound to be more carefully watched. As an aristocrat, he did not have much confidence in the branch elected by the people.

But that aristocratic-democrat, George Mason of Virginia, disagreed. "The first branch should be given the taxing power because it will be made up of the immediate representatives of the people. The second will not. Therefore, if the second branch has the power of giving away the people's money, the members of this branch may soon forget where the money came from. We might soon have tyranny."

James Wilson showed his intellectual impatience for what he considered a petty detail. "What difference does it make in which branch money bills originate, if both branches must agree in the end?"

Wilson had no sooner made this comment than he found himself in the strange position of seeming to carry on a debate against himself in front of the entire Convention. He had earlier offered to assist Benjamin Franklin by reading the old man's written comments to the delegates. Now Franklin handed him a sheet of paper and Wilson heard himself read words opposing his own statement: "It is of great importance that the people should know who has spent their money and how it has been spent. The best and only way to do this is to leave money affairs to the immediate representatives of the people. And if you cannot decide on the role of the second branch in money matters, perhaps you ought to reconsider my original idea of a legislature of one branch only."

Pausing long enough to take a sharp breath, Wilson told the delegates that now he wished to answer Dr. Franklin's words, which he had just read. "I approve of my colleague's principle of keeping the people informed on their own money affairs. But I believe that they would know as much and be as well-satisfied whichever branch of the legislature is given the power to originate money bills."

The discussion continued for days, with everyone becoming exhausted. Finally, all they could agree on was the appointment of a small committee to work out a new plan.

Just at this point the irrepressible Dr. Franklin shared an inspiration with everyone present: "I suggest that henceforth we have an opening prayer each morning, with one or more of this city's clergy officiating."

Stunned silence.

A difficult suggestion to oppose. Yet even more difficult to put into effect, as Alexander Hamilton pointed out diplomatically. "Dr. Franklin's proposal would have been quite in order at the very start of the Convention. However, to institute such prayer at this late date would lead the public to believe that constant dissension had made such a measure necessary."

A murmur of agreement made its way through the hall. Then the always practical Dr. Hugh Williamson of North Carolina blurted out, "Besides, we have no funds to pay a preacher."

This was the clinching argument. Without another word the Convention bypassed the whole issue by adjourning for the day.

CHAPTER SIX

WITH LITTLE or no hard news from the Convention, the newspapers sometimes contented their readers with wild rumors. So wild, in fact, that the delegates often suspected the publishers of trying to provoke them into breaking the rule of secrecy.

Philadelphia's leading newspaper, the *Pennsylvania Gazette*, printed without comment a detailed report current in New England. Preparations were well under way, the editors claimed, for importing Frederick, Duke of York, second son of King George III of England. Frederick would then be crowned king of the infant United States. Of course, there would first have to be a suitable apology by the United States for her recent terrible behavior toward England!

The report caused many tears at the Convention—tears of frustration and tears of laughter. But the report also had the effect of causing the delegates to work even harder and faster. They had given the country a legislature with

two branches, but in outline form. Now they had to work on small but essential details.

Terms of office, for example. Should they be the same for both houses? No, they finally concluded. Shorter terms for the House of Representatives, as they now called the first branch, than for the Senate or second branch.

"One-year terms are long enough for the House of Representatives," stammered Elbridge Gerry of Massachusetts.

"Annual elections are the only defense of the people against tyranny. The House is to be the voice of the people. Therefore the people must be able to express their approval or disapproval frequently."

"I disagree," argued James Madison. "At the very minimum the term should be three years. It will take at least that long for representatives to get to know the needs of states other than their own. And travel takes so long that only states close to the capital will be well-represented if the term is just one year."

"You are wrong, Mr. Madison. Elbridge Gerry is absolutely right." This from Connecticut's Roger Sherman, who saw great danger in terms longer than one year. "If representatives stay at the seat of government for any great length of time, they will acquire habits of the place which might differ from those of the people who voted for them."

Alexander Hamilton surprised no one by supporting as few elections as possible. "If elections are held too frequently, the people lose interest and do not bother to vote. Then the small number who do bother to vote can control the country."

In the end the delegates agreed on two-year terms for the House of Representatives and turned to the term of office for senators. Suggestions varied from appointment for life terms to an unlimited number of terms of four years to a single seven-year term.

James Wilson of Pennsylvania voiced his usual carefully reasoned ideas. He reminded the delegates that foreign nations had so far refused to do business with the United States because "they have had up till now no confidence in the stability or workability of our government."

Jabbing the air with his fist for emphasis, Wilson insisted: "Nine years with a rotation for Senate members will make the Senate respectable in the eyes of the world. And there is an added advantage: Our government will then be far superior to foreign monarchies, which are dependent by their very nature on the temper of one man.

"Do not fear that a nine-year term will encourage senators to vote themselves terms for life. The answer to this objection, of course, is having one third of the terms expire every three years. In this way there will always be three divisions holding their places for unequal terms and therefore acting under the influence of different views and different impulses."

The delegates thought the idea of rotations ingenious, but balked at a term as long as nine years. Nor could they agree with the much shorter four-year term proposed by General Charles Cotesworth Pinckney, a Revolutionary war hero, South Carolina lawyer, and cousin of his state's other Charles Pinckney. Without apology he borrowed the words Roger Sherman had used in his speech favoring a short term for the House of Representatives. He argued that a nine-year-term would keep senators away from home for so long a period that they would become more familiar with the nation's capital than with the state they were supposedly representing.

Governor Randolph of Virginia preferred seven years if a means of rotation could be worked out. This suggested to the always practical Dr. Hugh Williamson of North Carolina a term of six years: "Only one year less, but much more convenient for rotation."

By a favorable vote of seven to four—with New York,

New Jersey, South Carolina, and Georgia in opposition—the Convention voted a six-year term for the Senate, with one third to be rotated every two years.

Next they turned to the issue of salaries. Should these be high enough to attract the best possible men in the country? Or was Benjamin Franklin right in thinking that absolutely no salary should be paid to government officials, that the dignity and prestige of governmental office were more than enough compensation?

The arguments came thick and fast. With no salary, only the wealthiest could afford to serve. Only the wealthiest, therefore, would be represented.

But if the salaries were to be as high as suggested, should the states pay their own representatives or should the national government provide the money? If the states had to assume this burden, might not the less wealthy states soon find themselves without sufficient representation? Equally displeasing, if the national government paid their salaries, might the representatives not find themselves beholden to that government rather than to their own state?

Again there were more problems than solutions, and again the matter was referred to a special committee for further study and suggestion.

The delegates also indicated a willingness to leave other details—for instance, qualifications of age and residence—to the same committee. Debate by the entire Convention, even meeting as the Committee of the Whole, had to be reserved for major questions only.

CHAPTER SEVEN

THE DELEGATES could no longer avoid the issue of how the states should be represented in the national legislature. As a result, in the meetings of the Committee of the Whole there were constant quarrels, accompanied by threats to dissolve the Convention completely.

Outlandish schemes for settling the dispute consumed a great deal of time. There was the day that Judge George Read of Delaware, the smallest state at the Convention, suggested getting rid of the states altogether. "Every argument about representation and power for the national legislature comes down to the small states versus the large states. We would be far better off to unite into one great society without local boundaries."

Judge Read claimed special prestige as one of the eight Convention delegates who had signed the Declaration of Independence. Even so, nobody bothered to suggest a vote on this idea.

On another day Benjamin Franklin went so far as to offer parts of his own state of Pennsylvania to New Jersey and Delaware. "Small states are easier to govern than large states. We should give part of the huge state of Pennsylvania to its small neighbors, Delaware and New Jersey, and thereby equal out the size of all three states. Other areas of the country could follow this example and then all thirteen states would be similar in size."

But Massachusetts and Virginia made no such offers, so a better answer had to be found. As usual, Virginia's most effective delegate, James Madison, went to the heart of the problem and stated it so that at the very least all delegates would be debating the same question: "Should we give the states any power at all, and if we do, how shall we keep some states from becoming more powerful than others?"

His fellow intellectual, James Wilson of Pennsylvania, thought he could see a partial answer. "All members of the national government will also be representatives of all the people of all the states. Therefore these members will find themselves obliged to give to the states whatever powers the people wish the states to keep."

Madison viewed this as indeed only a partial answer, and in a long speech he explored the problem he himself had stated so well. "Frankly, I find less danger of tyranny from the general government than from the states. Under the Articles of Confederation the states often refused to heed the central government even when the good of the whole nation was at stake. But on the contrary, the central government would certainly never take power away from the states if this power was proved to be desirable for the people."

He continued with some emotion: "The state governments know about local problems. The central government is too far away and too busy to realize that these problems even exist, let alone knowing what to do about them. Therefore no reasonable person can object to giving states the powers over certain areas of government."

Then Madison came to his main point—tactfully but emphatically. "If we give the states too many powers or make them entirely independent of the national government, we have forgotten our main purpose in calling together this Convention—to avoid repeating the mistakes of the Articles of Confederation and thus bringing about absolute calamity."

However, Madison failed to convince Charles Pinckney of South Carolina, a veteran politician at the age of thirty who had already served two terms in the Congress of the Confederation. Now young Pinckney warned: "The general government must frequently depend on the states for their support and for carrying out the government's programs. Just for this reason alone the states must remain strong. And never forget, it is only through preserving the rights of the states that the rights of the people can be preserved."

William Pierce from the neighboring state of Georgia looked up from the notes he was taking on his fellow delegates to register a milder point of view. "State distinctions must be sacrificed as far as the general good requires, but without destroying the states."

Elbridge Gerry of Massachusetts, blurring for the moment his image as a strong supporter of states' rights, urged everyone to remember that even under the Confederation states were never completely independent. He demanded:

"End this petty squabbling and instead behave like a band of brothers, belonging to the same family."

At last Alexander Hamilton of New York spoke up. He had been silent until now, partly from respect to others whose age and experience made him unwilling to oppose them. He was also in the awkward position of being constantly outvoted by the two other members of the New York delegation, John Lansing and Robert Yates—with the result that his opinions carried no weight in his own state's votes. But the crisis had become too serious. He could no longer remain silent. In a speech as shocking as it was long, he proposed the strongest possible central government—patterned closely after the British government. "The British government is the best in the world and I doubt very much whether anything short of it will do in America.

"Under a strong government such as I propose, the small states would be more secure than they are with their equal voting rights under the Confederation. The more unified the country becomes, the more complete the authority of the government becomes, with less opportunity for the stronger states to injure the weaker ones. Remember, too, that Massachusetts, Pennsylvania, and Virginia are separated by hundreds of miles from each other and have few common interests. There should be no fear of their ever combining against the smaller states."

Hamilton's words on the three largest states were later picked up and elaborated by Madison, who like the others totally ignored the younger man's glorification of the British government: "In point of location the most jealous citizen of the most jealous state could not more effectively separate Massachusetts, Pennsylvania, and Virginia. In point

of manners, religion, and the other circumstances which sometimes cause affection to develop between different communities they are no more similar than the other states. In point of goods produced they are as different as any three other states in the Union. The chief product of Virginia is tobacco, of Pennsylvania flour, and of Massachusetts fish.

"These states may be alike in size but this has not made

them join together regularly in votes recorded by the Congress of the Confederation. History teaches that strong nations tend to be rivals rather than allies. Carthage and Rome tore one another to pieces instead of uniting their forces to devour the weaker nations of the earth. Austria and France were hostile as long as they remained the greatest powers of Europe. Now England and France have become the strongest powers and are enemies.

"We have but two choices: complete independence of each of the thirteen states, or complete unity as one nation. If all states become independent nations, the smaller states would have to fear military conquest by the larger. If instead there is complete unity under which all share common concern for the country and are subject to the same laws, the smaller states would have nothing to fear."

The speech contributed a great deal to the six-to-five vote in the Committee of the Whole, approving the Virginia Plan for proportional representation: The greater the population, the greater the number of representatives—in both branches of the legislature. The actual vote, recorded geographically from north to south, was Massachusetts, aye; Connecticut, no; New York, no; New Jersey, no; Pennsylvania, aye; Delaware, no; Maryland, no; Virginia, aye; North Carolina, aye; South Carolina, aye; Georgia, aye.

With such a narrow victory, the large states set about to win more support from their smaller neighbors for the final test—the vote in Convention Assembled. As an indication of goodwill they agreed to cease referring to the national government and to substitute the name The United

States, thereby subtly emphasizing the continuing importance of the states.

However, when the formal Convention reassembled on Wednesday, June 20, 1787, with George Washington once again in the President's chair, the rift between small and large factions became wider than ever. It was almost as though the Committee of the Whole had never met. The small states were determined and united in their opposition, and were strengthened in numbers daily by the arrival of additional delegates. They came up with their own set of resolutions, the New Jersey Plan, to counter what they considered absolutely unacceptable in the Virginia Plan.

75-10861
ENTRAL ARKANSAS LIBRARY SYSTEM
OOKMOBILE DEPARTMENT
00 LOUISIANA
TTLE ROCK, ARKANSAS

CHAPTER EIGHT

AGAIN DISCOURAGEMENT was in the air, with many delegates disgruntled at the undoing of almost three weeks of hard work in the Committee of the Whole. Alexander Hamilton, a strong advocate of proportional representation, went home in disgust after being constantly outvoted by his fellow New York delegates, John Lansing and Robert Yates, who favored equal representation. Hamilton told Washington that he could be summoned back to Philadelphia by letter if absolutely necessary, but found his continued presence a complete waste of time under the circumstances.

New Jersey took the floor to argue for giving all states equal representation in both legislative branches, regardless of the state's size or wealth. For one of her spokesmen she chose Jonathan Dayton, the youngest member of the Convention—to the considerable annoyance of many of the delegates, who considered his very presence an insult.

Dayton was twenty-seven years old and had served as a captain in the Revolutionary Army. However, his father still treated him like a naughty child, constantly led astray by bad friends. It was common gossip that the elder Dayton had arranged to have New Jersey send his son in his own place as a delegate to the Constitutional Convention. Brilliant solution, the father continually boasted. Now the friends would be far enough away during the entire summer and he, the father, could go on tending to the prosperous family business.

And so Jonathan Dayton went down in history as one of the fifty-five men responsible for the Constitution, while his father was largely ignored or sometimes mentioned in passing as a close relative of a famous man. Dayton turned out to be a conscientious delegate, although several members of the Convention remained decidedly cool to him.

William Paterson and David Brearley, also New Jersey delegates, joined their younger colleague in pleading for the New Jersey Plan for equal representation. As chief spokesman, Paterson complained that Virginia's Plan had received a barely favorable vote in the Committee of the Whole not because of merit but simply because it was the first to be presented. He asked pointedly: "What, pray tell me, is representation based on numbers? Shall I submit the welfare of New Jersey with five votes in a council where Virginia has sixteen? No! Neither my state nor myself will ever submit to despotism or to tyranny."

Judge Brearly used a more subtle approach. He moved that George Washington write to New Hampshire. "We must inform that state that the business now before the Convention is of such nature as to require attendance of its deputies. The difficulties of the subject under discussion and the difference of opinion call for all the assistance we can possibly obtain."

Of course, the large states and their Southern allies strongly protested this motion as an attempt to add to small-state strength. Former Governor John Rutledge of South Carolina observed: "They already know of the Convention and can attend if they choose. Rhode Island may as well be urged to appoint and send deputies. Are we to suspend business until New Hampshire's deputies arrive?"

Rufus King of Massachusetts noted: "I have written more than once as a private correspondent and the answers have given me every reason to expect that New Hampshire will be represented very shortly. Circumstances of a personal nature—lack of funds—have prevented it up till now. A letter could have no effect."

James Wilson of Pennsylvania said: "Would it be consistent with the rule or reason of secrecy to communicate to New Hampshire that the business is as urgent as the motion describes? It would spread a great alarm. Besides, I doubt that it is proper to solicit any state. This meeting is purely voluntary."

It was easy enough to defeat the motion on sending a special letter to New Hampshire. But it was becoming painfully obvious that it would be impossible to win final delegate support for either the large states' plan of proportional representation in each legislative branch or the small states' plan of equal representation.

Benjamin Franklin expressed the dilemma very well. "The difference of opinion turns on two points. If proportional representation takes place, the small states contend that their liberties will be in danger. If an equality of votes is to be put in its place, the large states say their money will be in danger."

He concluded: "When a broad table is to be made and the edges of planks do not fit, the artist takes a little from both and makes a good joint. In like manner here both sides must part with some of their demands, in order that they may join in some accommodating proposition."

Connecticut now took the lead in presenting just such a compromise: representation by population in the House of Representatives and equal representation in the Senate.

The small states were delighted. Equal votes in one branch of the legislature should be enough, they thought, to restrain the branch dominated by the large states.

But there were ominous rumblings of discontent from the large states. They saw no reason to go back on the victory, so dearly won in the Committee of the Whole, providing proportional representation in both branches. They were angered at the threats of the small states to abandon the Convention if the Connecticut Compromise, as it was now being called, did not win enough votes.

Several delegates from large states gave strong speeches of denunciation. James Wilson of Pennsylvania made it unmistakably clear that he wanted no part of the Connecticut Compromise. "Can we forget for whom we are forming a government? Is it for *men*, or for the imaginary beings called *states*? Representation ought on every principle to be the same in the second as in the first branch. If the government is not based on this foundation, it can be neither solid nor lasting.

"The United States at present groans under the weakness and inefficiency of its government. To remedy this weakness we have been sent to this Convention. If the compromise should be agreed to, we shall leave the United States bound precisely as before, with the additional difficulty of seeing the good purposes of the fair representation of the people in the first branch defeated in the second."

In his own mild but scholarly way James Madison now shocked the Convention. "The wrong issue is being considered. The states are divided into different interests not by the difference in size or population but by the effects of their having or not having slaves. There is only one way to solve this problem. In one branch states should be represented according to the number of free inhabitants only. In the other branch they should be represented according to the whole number, counting the slaves as if free. By this arrangement Southern states would have the advantage in one branch and the Northern in the other."

But for once the delegates ignored James Madison. His startling suggestion had no immediate effect on the men of the Convention, restless and weary because of the unbearably hot weather and long angry debates.

In the interest of reaching *some* agreement, the delegates decided to separate the Connecticut Compromise into two parts—the method of representation in the first branch and the method of representation in the second branch. By exactly the same vote as in the Committee of the Whole, they again approved of representation according to population in the House of Representatives, the first branch. On this part of the plan there was no difference anyway between Virginia and Connecticut.

When they came to a vote on equal representation of all states in the Senate the result was a tie. Previously, in the Committee of the Whole, the vote on this same issue had been six-to-five in favor. Dramatically, at the last possible moment, thirty-three-year-old Abraham Baldwin, a former Connecticut resident who was now considered Georgia's ablest lawyer, changed his vote to favor the Connecticut Compromise. Since only two Georgia members, Baldwin and William Houstoun, were present and voting at this time, the one-to-one division canceled Georgia's vote, much to the relief of Baldwin. He had feared the deliberate departure of the small states—and thus the end of the Convention—should they lose on this issue now.

Again the delegates saw no other way but to give the dispute to a committee to work out an agreeable compromise—in this case, the committee already charged with considering the origin of money bills. A small group, they hoped, would be both efficient and effective. Besides, July 4 with all its gala events was upon them, and they convinced themselves that they deserved time off for fun and relaxation.

CHAPTER NINE

MORE BAD moments. The issue of slavery, successfully ignored when brought up previously by James Madison, now demanded full-scale debate. And at this worst possible time, when divisiveness had reached such bitter depths, Robert Yates and John Lansing, personal friends and lawyers from Albany, New York, chose to launch their scheme to wreck the Convention forever.

They left Philadelphia abruptly after announcing their intention to return home for good because the Convention was going far beyond the power—delegated by the Congress of the Confederation—to revise the Articles of Confederation. New York State, they contended, would never authorize its delegates to exceed these original instructions. The two Albany lawyers never doubted that the small states would unhesitatingly follow their lead.

But almost immediately a boomerang effect set in. At the same time that Yates and Lansing were departing, Maryland's third delegate, Daniel Carroll, arrived on the scene. Always interested in establishing a stable government, Carroll had signed the original Articles of Confederation and now would agree to compromise for the sake of an effective Constitution. So New York was lost for the small states, and Maryland, instead of having a divided vote, would split two-to-one in favor of a well-organized national government. A double gain.

Meanwhile, discouraged by the constant discord, George Washington dispatched a letter to Alexander Hamilton—a letter that he made no effort to keep secret: "Please return as soon as possible. We can no longer spare your vigorous nationalist support. I am bitterly disappointed in those delegates who oppose a strong and energetic government. They are nothing more than narrow-minded politicians who allow local considerations to overshadow the good of the entire nation."

Recoiling at being considered "narrow-minded politicians," many delegates took a new look at themselves and at the nation's future. They concluded that they absolutely had to produce a new Constitution, even though there were bound to be features with which every delegate could and would find fault. The alternative was unthinkable: the downfall of the United States, followed by foreign takeover.

In this new mood the delegates no longer put off discussing even the most sensitive issues. While the special committee worked on the problems of origin of money bills and of equal or proportional representation for the Senate, the delegates decided that slavery or blacks or property—however they referred to it—should be discussed now. Several Southern states had suggested basing representation on wealth as well as on population. And for these states, without question, wealth and slavery were the same.

For many delegates, listing slaves as a state's wealth was wrong. Yet when they discussed how they were to consider slaves—as part of a state's wealth or as part of its population—they found the question complicated, the answers endless.

Plunging into the argument over whether slaves were men or property, William Paterson, chief spokesman for the New Jersey Plan and an able and knowledgeable debater, exclaimed: "Slaves are not free agents, have no personal liberty, cannot themselves acquire property. They are

themselves property, and like other property are entirely at the will of their master."

He went on to examine the purpose of representation and found it a substitute for the inconvenience of a meeting by the people themselves—"in the form of an assembly of certain individuals chosen by the people." And then clinching his argument on the status of slaves, he said: "If such a meeting of all the people were actually to take place, would the slaves vote? I assure you they would not. Why then should they be represented?"

Hardly waiting for Paterson to take his seat, Pierce But-

ler of South Carolina answered heatedly: "Because to be fair the Convention must consider wealth in apportioning representation. And never forget that for the South the slaves are wealth."

Rufus King of Massachusetts, a thirty-two-year-old Harvard-educated lawyer, now took the floor. A supporter of strong nationalist government, and possessed of considerable oratorical and legal talents, he was willing to settle for less than perfection to assure a new Constitution. "There is ample ground for compromise here. The Southern states are the richest. They cannot be expected to ally themselves with the North unless some attention is paid to their greater wealth—their slaves.

"The North, on the other hand, has the largest population of freemen and needs protection for its citizens and for commerce, which is their livelihood. Therefore, count the South's slaves for purposes of both taxation and represenation. This would at one and the same time grant the North some relief from taxes and give the South a broader base for representation in Congress."

However, South Carolina in the persons of Pierce Butler and forty-year-old General Charles Cotesworth Pinckney—a more brilliant thinker but not as good a speaker as his younger cousin Charles Pinckney—ignored all talk of compromise. For the better part of that week of July 9, they insisted that blacks be included equally with whites in determining representation. But they carefully avoided the issue of taxation.

To counter South Carolina's stand, and in opposition to the proposal of their colleague Rufus King, Massachusetts' delegates Elbridge Gerry and Nathaniel Gorham suggested counting three fifths of each state's slaves—plus the total number of freemen—in determining representation and taxation.

Pierce Butler retorted: "The labor of a slave in South Carolina is as productive and valuable as that of a freeman in Massachusetts. Since wealth is needed for defense and for paying expenses of government, slaves are as valuable to the nation as freemen are. Consequently, equal represenation ought to be allowed for slaves in a government set up principally for the protection of property and indeed supported by property."

Now that rebellious Southerner, George Mason of Virginia, rose to protest: "Slaves are useful to the community at large, but I refuse to regard slaves as equal to freemen. I will not vote to include them as such for purposes of representation."

Dr. Hugh Williamson, North Carolina's practical but tireless debater, rejected both Northern and Southern extremists: "The Southern states insist that blacks are inferior to whites—when taxation is considered. And of course the North, especially the Eastern states, insists that slaves are equal to freemen—when it comes to taxation. I myself approve of the ratio of three fifths."

At this point Pierce Butler moved formally to consider blacks as equal to whites in the apportionment of representation. Of the ten states present, only Delaware, South Carolina, and Georgia voted in favor, so the motion was defeated.

As the debate resumed, Gouverneur Morris of Pennsylvania injected a pointed question. "If slaves are to be considered as wealth, then why is no other wealth but slaves included?"

He paused briefly, then continued. "And there is another objection against including slaves in the number counted for representation—the people of my state of Pennsylvania would revolt at the idea of being put on a footing with slaves. They would reject any plan that was to have such an effect."

His fellow Pennsylvanian James Wilson, an early supporter of human rights who had signed the Declaration of Independence, carried the thought further. "On what principle can anyone explain the admission of blacks in the proportion of three fifths? Are they admitted as citiizens? Then why are they not admitted on an equality with white citizens? Are they admitted as property? Then why is no other property counted?"

William Davie, thirty-year-old lawyer from North Carolina, was furious and made no attempt to hide his feelings. "It is high time to speak out. Some gentlemen intend to deprive the Southern states of any share of representation for their blacks. I am sure that my state will never join the Union on any terms that do not count at least three fifths of the blacks. If the Eastern states mean to exlude the blacks altogether, this Convention is at an end."

Bowing to this threat, the delegates finally settled on a compromise. Taxes and representation would be based on the number of each state's "free persons" plus three fifths of "all other persons." An actual count of both categories would be taken within three years after the first meeting of the new Congress of the United States, and within every ten years afterward.

Quite willingly, Southerners spared the feelings of some Northerners by keeping the words "slave," "Negro," and "blacks" out of the sacred document of the Constitution. But no matter what those newfangled books known as dictionaries said, everyone had to acknowledge that "all other persons" in this instance referred to slaves.

For various reasons the votes of five of the thirteen states were not included on this new compromise regarding taxes and representation. Massachusetts and South Carolina were present, but divided. New Hampshire's delegates still had not arrived, although rumor had it that they were finally en route. Rhode Island was still ignoring the Convention. New York would remain unrepresented for several more weeks—while George Washington's letter made its way slowly to New York and Alexander Hamilton prepared for and made the journey back to Philadelphia.

Of the other eight states New Jersey and Delaware voted no. Six voted aye: Connecticut, Pennsylvania, Maryland, Virginia, North Carolina, and Georgia. The issue turned out not to be between North and South, or even between large and small states.

The delegates saw themselves as real fathers, giving one thing to certain members of the family to make up for something given to the rest of the family. They had become convinced that the only way to build a better future was to ensure a beginning—even one far from perfect.

CHAPTER TEN

SWEET REASON was in the air. But if the delegates had expected praise, or even a relaxation in formality, from their chairman George Washington, they were disappointed. Even dismayed.

Holding back a motion for adjournment, Washington flung a sheaf of papers onto his desk. "Will the owner of these notes on Convention proceedings please step forward to claim them at once! They were left in the hall after adjournment yesterday."

Absolute silence. Not a single movement.

After a suitable pause, Washington continued with teeth clenched, lips pursed: "I must entreat every gentleman present to be more careful lest our business get into newspapers and disturb the public by premature speculation."

Then Washington bowed stiffly, picked up his hat and, as Major Pierce of Georgia noted in his diary, left the room with a dignity so severe that everyone present seemed alarmed. Not a single person ever made a move to claim the notes as his own. Nor was the mistake ever repeated.

The incident underlined the crisis atmosphere of the

Convention. Delegates had to press forward with never the slightest relaxation in their rules of procedure, never any self-congratulation—even for resolving the most divisive issues.

And so later that same week they moved on to the issue of representation in the Senate. It was Friday and it was the thirteenth, but they had time neither for superstition nor for a long weekend.

The committee chosen earlier to work out a compromise made its report. Their recommendation: Money bills should originate in the House of Representatives and there should be equality of votes in the Senate.

Reaction was immediate. Roger Sherman of Connecticut liked the plan and wanted no changes made. He begged: "Do not start the debate again. It is a conciliatory plan, and a great deal of time and thought have already gone into it."

Luther Martin, a Princeton-educated Maryland lawyer, agreed. "Let us vote at once. I do not like the inequality of votes in the House of Representatives, but I am willing to try the plan rather than do nothing."

Then he added defiantly: "Let the large states leave the Union if they do not like the plan. I would rather there should be two unions than one founded on any other principle than an equality of votes, in the second branch at least."

Young Charles Pinckney of South Carolina continued to object to equal votes in the Senate, and went so far as to suggest exact numbers of senators for each state, based on an estimate of their populations. New Hampshire would have two members, Massachusetts four, Rhode Island one, Connecticut three, New York three, New Jersey two, Pennsylvania four, Delaware one, Maryland three, Virginia five, North Carolina three, South Carolina three, Georgia two— for a total of thirty-six senators.

James Wilson of Pennsylvania seconded the motion at once.

Jonathan Dayton of New Jersey, the Convention's youngest delegate, argued against it. "The smaller states can never give up their equality. Otherwise they cannot protect their rights."

Judge Roger Sherman of Connecticut objected in his Yankee accent. "There must be equality of votes in order to protect the state governments. Only if state governments are represented will they have a means of restraining the national government."

But James Madison from his writing desk at the front of the hall supported Pinckney's motion as a reasonable compromise.

And Rufus King, Massachusetts' great orator, saw no clear reason why the same rule of representation should not prevail in the second branch as in the first. To provide security for state governments, he suggested three branches of the legislature. "The second was admitted to be necessary and was actually meant to check the first branch, to give more wisdom and stability to the government. Since its actions are going to affect the people, it ought to be proportioned to the numbers of people. For the third purpose of securing the states, there ought then to be a third branch, representing the states as such and guarding by equal votes their rights and dignities."

Here King became emotional as he fairly shouted: "No government can last that is not founded on just principles. I prefer doing nothing to allowing an equal vote to all the states. It would be better to submit to a little more confusion and convulsion under the Articles of Confederation, than to submit to such an evil under a new Constitution."

His Massachusetts colleague, Caleb Strong, partially blind as a result of smallpox, considered himself a representative of his state's rural residents and took an opposite view. "If we do not come to agreement, the Union itself must soon be dissolved. The small states have made a considerable concession in the Committee report by agreeing to have all money bills originate in the House of Representatives, which will be controlled by the large states. Now the small states naturally expect some concessions on the other side. Therefore, I am compelled to give my vote for the Committee report taken as a whole."

James Madison continued to voice strong exception to the Committee report. "If the proper foundation of government is destroyed, by substituting an equality in place of a proportional representation, no proper superstructure will be raised. No one will say that either in the Congress of the Confederation or in the nation Delaware has had equal weight with Pennsylvania. If Pennsylvania supplied ten times as much money as Delaware, then it would be ten times more important. Even if there is proportional representation in the House of Representatives, an equality of votes in the Senate will mean that a minority can defeat the will of the majority of the people."

James Wilson of Pennsylvania denounced equality of representation in the Senate as an error that time would never correct, an error so basic as to be avoided by all means. "I admit that the states ought to be preserved. But does it follow that an equality of votes is necessary for the purpose? The present Congress, in which states are represented equally, has the great fault of inactivity. We were sent here to remedy that fault. What will we answer when the people ask why we have given them a government that is more complicated than the one they have now, but has all its weaknesses?"

In line with all these arguments, young Charles Pinckney of South Carolina repeated his proposal for representation in the Senate—with numbers ranging from five votes for Virginia, the state with the largest population, to three for his own state and one for Delaware, the smallest state present. Late Saturday afternoon the Convention roundly defeated Pinckney's plan. Then, exhausted, the delegates adjourned for the weekend.

First thing Monday they resumed voting on the Committee's recommendations: equal representation in the Senate and origin of money bills in the House of Representatives. The outcome held everyone in suspense right up to Georgia, the last state to be recorded. The final tally was five states in favor and four opposed, with Massachusetts divided. New York's delegates had all departed, so that representation at the Convention took a step backward—from eleven states present to only ten.

A change of one vote in the Massachusetts delegation could have brought about a Convention tie and defeat of the Committee compromise. Of the four Massachusetts delegates, Elbridge Gerry and Caleb Strong supported the Committee, while Nathaniel Gorham fought against it. In the course of the debate Rufus King was unexpectedly persuaded to join his colleague Gorham. Had either Gerry or Strong been similarly persuaded to join King and Gorham, Massachusetts would have been recorded against the compromise—with a resultant ineffective tie vote of five states opposed and five in favor. Then, without doubt, the small states would have carried out their threat to leave the Convention for good.

For the future, Madison's prophecy of North versus South might hold true, but for the present the vote was decided on the basis of the votes of five small states: Connecticut, New Jersey, Delaware, Maryland and North Carolina voted aye. Two other small (and Southern) states, South Carolina and Georgia, voted no, along with two large states, Pennsylvania and Virginia.

CHAPTER ELEVEN

Now INDEPENDENCE HALL was the scene of bitter suggestions by delegates whose very appearance symbolized the size of their states—Edmund Randolph, the extremely tall governor of Virginia, and William Paterson, the diminutive lawyer of New Jersey.

"Adjourn this Convention immediately," Randolph demanded. "We have gone too far in compromising representation in Congress. I for one would never have agreed to making the Senate so powerful if I had believed we would go so far as to give all states, regardless of wealth or population, the same vote. Preposterous!"

"I would go one step further," said Paterson, his voice strained with anger. "Let us adjourn, return home and above all, get rid of this cursed rule of secrecy. We owe it to the people we represent to tell them of our decisions. Our state may have conceded too much on proportional representation for the House of Representatives."

General Charles Cotesworth Pinckney of South Carolina, whose words always seemed to command respect, interjected: "Going home before finishing our business is ridiculous. I cannot even consider going back to South Carolina and then returning to Philadelphia. You do not say if you mean to adjourn without setting a time for a new meeting. But if you do mean this, you are putting an end to the Convention forever."

Now, without warning, the delegates were stunned to catch sight of a large glass bottle containing a two-headed snake preserved in liquid. It turned out to be a gift to Benjamin Franklin from one of his many scientific friends. With a twinkle that old pacifier asked: "What would happen if the snake were still alive and one head decided to go in one direction while the other head decided just as strongly to go the opposite way?"

Everyone at the Convention got the point. Randolph and Paterson both reconsidered. Randolph moved to adjourn for one day only. Paterson seconded the motion. Even this watered-down version of an attempt to display disapproval by an act of adjournment passed with difficulty, after first being defeated by a tie vote.

Leaving the hall, the delegates from the large states agreed informally to use the extra time to their own advantage. They would meet by themselves for the rest of the day in the hope of uniting on a new plan of legislative representation.

But they had no success. They hesitated to take any action that might conceivably cause the collapse of the Convention. They decided to do nothing to change the close vote on the compromise. After the meeting Madison remarked with a smile, "This ought to satisfy the small states forever that they have nothing to fear from a conspiracy of the large states."

The following day the delegates settled down to the question of actual numbers of representatives in both legislative branches. For the House they assigned representatives from each state according to population, including three fifths of the slaves. But when they came to the number of senators from each state, they began a new round of controversy.

Gouverneur Morris of Pennsylvania, who spoke at least once on every subject, pleaded for three senators from each state. "The Senate ought to be a large body of men. If only two members are allowed to each state and a majority vote should be allowed, the power would be lodged in fourteen members. Too small a number for so much power."

George Mason, Virginia's elder statesman and powerful speaker, reminded the delegates that new states would soon be entering the Union. "Three senators from each state would be far too many to work efficiently. And the additional expense seems quite unnecessary."

The practicality of this idea impressed North Carolina's Dr. Hugh Williamson, who agreed. "If the number is too great, the distant states will not be on an equal footing with the nearer states who can more easily send and support their ablest citizens."

Those who favored two senators per state finally won out. They received an unexpected vote with the arrival of New Hampshire's delegates, John Langdon, forty-six and a wealthy merchant, and Nicholas Gilman, a thirty-two-year-old lawyer. Langdon, impatient to have New Hampshire represented at the Convention and anxious to be chosen a delegate, had supplied the necessary money from his own funds.

Taking advantage of the glow of agreement, the Convention quickly moved on to decide that each senator and member of the House of Representatives should vote as an individual, rather than as part of a state unit. The delegates thus approved a radical departure from the method of voting in the Congress of the Confederation or in the Convention itself. In both assemblies, states' votes frequently did not count because of a tie vote within the delegation. Or equally objectionable, opposing members' votes often went unnoticed because they were in the minority of their own state delegation.

After spending two full months on the legislature, the delegates took a moment—no more—to indulge in self-satisfaction. They were extremely proud of their accomplishment; they had reached an agreeable compromise and at the same time successfully avoided a complete collapse of the Convention.

CHAPTER TWELVE

ALMOST JOYFULLY the Convention turned to a new phase of the Constitution—the executive branch. Here they could be creative to their heart's content. Under the Articles of Confederation the country had had no executive. People often referred to a "president" of the Congress of the Confederation, but he was just the presiding officer at meetings of that body, much as George Washington was the presiding officer of the Convention. The chaos and lack of centralized authority resulting from the failure to give the nation a chief executive had contributed heavily to the calling of the present Convention.

No other country in the world had ever had an executive chosen by and responsive to the needs and wishes of the people. The delegates decided on the title *President* for the nation's executive, suggested by the term in use for the heads of state of Pennsylvania, Delaware, New Jersey, and New Hampshire.

They gave very little time or space in the Constitution to the President. This was rather surprising. After all, under the doctrine of separation of powers into legislative, executive and judicial branches of government, he and the Vice President—whose major function was to succeed him in the event of death or inability to govern—were an entire branch of government.

But the delegates were human. And building on their own experiences, they could remember only the grief caused them by the tyranny of the British parliament and by the ineffectiveness of their own Congress of the Confederation. And so they had planned a new legislature down to the last detail to avoid the extremes of their two previous legislative experiences.

They had had little experience, however, with an executive. The British king and prime minister were dominated by parliament and so remained largely in the background of the American colonies' relationship with the British government. Therefore, the delegates were willing to deal in few specifics and many generalities for the executive branch. They would let time fill in the details.

The very newness of the title *President* set the tone of debate. Nothing about the young country's executive was to be like the monarchs of the Old World.

Dr. Hugh Williamson of North Carolina led off the discussion by gently denouncing all suggestions of a life term for the President. "Reluctantly I will go along with the sense of the Convention that we have one, instead of two or three, executives. But I fear that a single executive will be nothing more than an elective king. He will spare no pains to keep himself in for life and to ensure that his children succeed him.

"Therefore, I strongly favor limiting the President to a

single term, lasting a minimum of seven years and a maximum of twelve years."

Luther Martin of Maryland and Elbridge Gerry of Massachusetts, both usually known for dull, wordy speeches, agreed quickly for once.

But Connecticut Judge Oliver Ellsworth, a powerful debater, swayed many with his reminder that all humans desire reward and recognition for their best efforts. "The Executive should be reelected if his conduct proves him worthy of it. And he will be more likely to render himself worthy of it if he may be rewarded by the possibility of reelection for more than one term. Our greatest men will be more willing to accept the office under this condition than if they foresee being degraded to ordinary citizen at a fixed period."

Rufus King of Massachusetts, advocate of a strong national government, agreed. "Make the President reeligible. Better to provide for impeachment by the legislature if he becomes too authoritarian than to give up the great advantage, noted by Mr. Ellsworth, in allowing the country to register approval by reelection."

For the moment the Convention reached no conclusion on reeligibility. Instead, they dealt with the length of term, and suggestions almost flew around the hall.

"Seven years," argued Hugh Williamson, the gentlemanly doctor from North Carolina.

"Eleven years," countered Luther Martin of Maryland.

"No, fifteen years, snorted Elbridge Gerry in such a firm and arrogant tone that, of course, his better-humored and popular rival Rufus King went him better: "Twenty years. This is the median life of princes."

"Too long," objected William Davie of North Carolina in his best courtroom manner. "Eight years."

"Nonsense," disagreed scholarly James Wilson. "If the executive should come into office at the age of thirty-five and his term should be fixed at fifteen years, then at the age of fifty, in the very prime of life and with all the aid of experience, he must be cast aside like a useless hulk."

His fellow Pennsylvanian Gouverneur Morris now rose to make another of his long and thoughtful speeches, in

Daniel Carroll

Robert Morris

Charles Pinckney

which he warned: "Make the President too weak and the legislature will usurp his powers. Make him too strong and he will usurp the legislature's powers. For myself, I prefer a short term of office, reeligibilty, and a method of election that will ensure having the best available man in office."

Following Morris' speech, two methods were most frequently suggested: election of the executive by the national legislature, or by electors appointed by the legislatures of the states for that purpose.

One other method, direct election by the people, was proposed. However, only Pennsylvania went on record as favoring popular election, although many prominent delegates, including James Madison, supported this method.

In a formal address to the Convention, Madison objected strongly to the appointment of the President by Congress. "This method would make the executive too dependent on the legislature, and the public interest would materially suffer. Worse still, the candidate might intrigue with the legislature to obtain his own appointment from the most powerful group. He would then be under obligation to do whatever this group asked.

"No, there are only two choices—appointment by electors chosen by the people, or an immediate appointment by the people. With all its imperfections, I prefer choice by the people."

Elbridge Gerry of Massachusetts, remembered for his stubborn support of equal representation in the Senate, despite his state's huge population, leapt to his feet at Madison's admission of "imperfections" in the method of popular election. "The people are too little informed of personal characteristics of leaders to make a wise decision."

And along these same lines George Mason of Virginia, whose aristocratic background overcame his democratic tendencies in this instance, added: "The extent of the country renders it impossible that the people can have the ability to judge the qualifications of the various candidates. Popular election would result in having the people led by a few men acting for their own selfish purposes." Young Charles Pinckney of South Carolina and Dr. Hugh Williamson of North Carolina voiced complete agreement.

Pierce Butler of South Carolina, acting to preserve Southern fortunes and traditions, just as he had done in the debate on counting slaves for representation, raised still another objection. He reminded everyone that the states had to be given a more important role in the election of the President than the role given to the people at large. "I prefer an election by electors chosen by the legislatures of the states. And each state must have an equal vote. We departed from this principle in the case of the legislature. But there is no reason for doing so in the case of the executive."

Disturbed at the turn of debate, Benjamin Franklin received special permission from George Washington to remain seated as he pleaded in his quavering voice: "It seems to have been imagined by some that depending on election by the mass of the people is degrading to the President. But in free government the rulers are the servants, and the people their superiors and sovereigns. For the rulers, therefore, to be dependent for election on the people is not to *degrade* but to *promote* them." (And here he tapped his cane for emphasis.)

Once again deadlock threatened. Each new vote undid

the previous vote. Finally the delegates agreed that constant disagreement over the executive branch made referral to committee absolutely essential.

But at least the debate had established a solid framework within which the committee could compromise and work out details. Everyone present agreed that the length of term should depend completely on the method of election. Thus, if the national legislature made the choice, the delegates would support a long term with no possibility of reelection. On the other hand, if the people or the state legislatures were to choose the President, the delegates would favor a shorter term and possible reelection.

Gratefully, the Convention seized on a motion to appoint a five-man Committee of Detail and then to adjourn for ten days while this Committee worked on the problem of the executive and in fact drew up a document incorporating the results of all debates and votes so far. The Committee would be empowered to suggest further compromises and exact details for all three branches—legislative, which they had debated intensively; executive, on which they had spent less time; and judicial, so far hardly mentioned.

The delegates were aware that they were giving an unprecedented amount of power to the Committee of Detail. However, they reasoned that they had already, in both the Committee of the Whole and in Convention assembled, provided the framework within which this important new Committee would function. And five minds, they hoped, might come up with better answers than those of an entire Convention.

The five-member Committee would, of course, have to

submit their report to the entire Convention for final approval. Nonetheless, the delegates had enough political experience to realize that, as with all highly organized and detailed reports, any changes made by the full assembly

were bound to be minor ones. Especially when members of the Convention were impatient to return home.

Therefore, before handing over this tremendous power, the Convention worked carefully to select the Committee. Delegates made certain that all geographical sections were represented and took into consideration age, knowledge, and experience in the art of government. They chose two members from the North: wealthy, forty-nine-year-old Nathaniel Gorham of Massachusetts, who had presided over both the Congress of the Confederation and the Convention's own Committee of the Whole; and Oliver Ellsworth of Connecticut, forty-two, judge of the Connecticut Supreme Court and a prime mover in the Connecticut Compromise, which had given the states representation acording to population in the House and equal representation in the Senate. From the Middle States they chose Pennsylvania lawyer James Wilson, who at the age of forty-five had spent a lifetime studying every detail of every government throughout history. And from the South they chose Governor Edmund Randolph of Virginia, at thirty-four the youngest of the group, and spokesman for the Virginia Plan; and John Rutledge, at forty-eight a highly respected lawyer, who had once served as governor of South Carolina.

From adjournment at the end of Thursday, July 26, 1787, to reconvening on Monday morning, August 6, these five men worked while the rest of the delegates relaxed. The season was perfect for trout fishing and excursions to the surrounding countryside. Even the conscientious George Washington could hardly wait to get out of Philadelphia. In the company of Gouverneur Morris and his hosts, Mr. and Mrs. Robert Morris, he returned to nearby Valley Forge for the first time since spending the miserable winter of 1777 there with his troops.

No wonder in later years Judge Ellsworth told his grandson that the entire Constitution of the United States was drawn up by himself and the other members of the Committee of Detail—and in just eleven days!

CHAPTER THIRTEEN

A RIVALRY, literally a rivalry unto death, had developed between the Congress of the Confederation meeting in New York and the Constitutional Convention meeting in Philadelphia. The longer the Convention went on—with that "cursed rule of secrecy"—the angrier the members of Congress and their supporters in the country became. The mere existence of the Convention was a gnawing insult, and threat, to the Congress. And it was growing worse by the day.

But the Congress had great advantages over the Convention: The day-to-day problems of governing the infant United States went right on—and the Congress of the Confederation was still in charge. Besides, without a rule of secrecy the members were free to make the best use of publicity.

"Nonsense," supporters of the Confederation such as Patrick Henry would answer indignantly—and publicly—to those who complained that there was no difference between British tyranny and American anarchy and chaos.

"Patience," members of Congress would counsel, pointing out that it had taken the world more than 2,500 years to produce the Declaration of Independence and its accompanying government. "Why replace this government just because it has not reached perfection a mere eleven years after it has come into existence?"

Congress asserted that its mistakes were not beyond correction. And at least once they came up with a flawless accomplishment—for which the members felt they deserved great praise.

Long ago they had turned their attention to the land north and west of the Ohio River. This was land England had considered worthless and so had thrown in along with the Treaty of 1783. Now in this summer of 1787 while the Philadelphia Convention labored over the Constitution, the Congress in New York passed the Northwest Ordinance. With no colonial charters or traditions to guide them in setting up the government in the Northwest Territory, they had relied on the Declaration of Independence.

The Declaration had proclaimed, "All men are created equal." So be it. For the first time in a national document, this Northwest Ordinance of 1787, Congress proclaimed that there would be no slavery in the new territory.

The Declaration had proclaimed that governments are instituted to provide for their citizens' "life, liberty, and the pursuit of happiness." Therefore, Congress included provision for free public education: "Religion, morality, and knowledge being necessary to good government and the happiness of mankind, schools and the means of education shall forever be encouraged." They also provided for religious freedom and trial by jury.

The Declaration had proclaimed: "Governments are instituted among men, deriving their just powers from the consent of the governed." In line with this revolutionary and majestic pronouncement, Congress provided self-government for the new territories as soon as there was enough population to make this practical.

And more startling in a world where every newly acquired territory became an immediate colony, set up to benefit the mother country, Congress provided for the admission of each territory "to statehood on an *equal basis with the original thirteen states*." The only requirement was a population of sixty thousand free inhabitants.

In this way Congress provided for the eventual admission to statehood of Ohio, Indiana, Illinois, Michigan, and Wisconsin, and set the pattern to be followed in the future admission of new states.

An impressive accomplishment, but somewhat worrisome to the men in Philadelphia. Selfishly, some loathed the idea of having the world and the nation heap praise on their New York rivals. All too soon, they feared, there would be questioning of the very necessity for the Convention.

Philosophically, Southerners were not so sure that they wanted to introduce the principle of forbidding slavery before a new state could be admitted.

And some delegates from the Northeast, led by Gouverneur Morris and Nathaniel Gorham, wanted to write immediate provisions in the new Constitution to correct a terrible threat in this ordinance. They wanted to ensure that the Atlantic states—the original Thirteen Colonies—

would never lose power to the new states formed farther west.

So the Congress in New York succeeded in adding still another area of discord to be reconciled by the Committee of Detail—East versus West. If successful, the Convention would have the opportunity to show the country that its answers were better than those of the Confederation.

CHAPTER FOURTEEN

WITH ONLY five days of cool weather between the opening of the Convention and the end of August—including two Sundays—it sometimes seemed like the silly season. Thus in the midst of weighty debates on the report of the Committee of Detail, Colonel George Mason of Virginia suggested in all seriousness giving Congress the right to regulate the people's eating habits. But he got too little support— even his own state voted against the formal motion.

Now great solutions to great problems emerged. The formula for success consisted of three months of hard work by the whole Convention, *plus* ten days of concentrated effort by the five-man Committee of Detail, *plus* five weeks of further debate by the Convention.

Contrary to Judge Ellsworth's proud boast to his grandson about the overriding importance of the Committee of Detail, the work of the Convention proved so essential as to mean the difference between success and failure. True, the Committee supplied the details for the new Constitution —a preamble plus forty-three weighty sections. But the Convention had supplied the general philosophy. And in the end the Convention added many more details before giving final approval.

From August 6 until September 10, one week before final adjournment, the Convention debated the report of the Committee of Detail. Delegates were pleased—and relieved—to discover that the Committee had in fact used previously adopted resolutions of the Convention as their guidelines. But they were flabbergasted to realize that the Committee had also relied heavily on the much denounced Articles of Confederation.

In the proposed new Constitution the Committee retained everything that had worked in the Articles of Confederation. For example, with colonial experience in mind, Pennsylvania's James Wilson, whose superior knowledge made him dominant in the Committee, kept the exact wording from the Articles forbidding arrest of a member of Congress for anything said or done in legislative sessions. The power to pass laws was worthless, Wilson pointed out, if legislators could be threatened with arrest or imprisonment for speaking their minds or acting freely in the line of duty.

Also with colonial history in mind, the Committee had taken from the Articles the idea, if not the exact words, that "the Congress shall assemble at least once in every year." Most members could recall times in their youth when the king's governors had refused permission for meetings of colonial assemblies or legislatures.

The Committee threw out altogether or tried to improve whatever had proved unworkable in the Articles. Out of ignorance—or selfishness—states had too often passed laws harmful to other states or to the whole country. Or, for the same reasons, they had failed to pass helpful laws. Even in wartime they had not been generous or prompt in their contributions of money and manpower when the decision had been left to them on a voluntary basis. Thus, the Committee granted the national legislature the general power to pass laws for the interests of the entire nation—and the specific powers to levy taxes and raise an army.

And they granted power of the purse. Without hesitation the Committee had given this to the national legislature alone, because they considered the legislative branch most representative of the people. Purposely they elevated the legislature to the lofty responsibility of providing money to ensure smooth running of the government—or, by the device of withholding funds, to put a complete halt to attempted tyranny by any branch.

In place of the Articles' provision that legislators should be paid out of state treasuries, the Committee strongly recommended that the national treasury pay these salaries. When the Convention came to vote on this proposal of the Committee of Detail, it turned out that there was no objection in the case of the House of Representatives. But, surprisingly, heated debate broke out in the case of the Senate.

Luther Martin and Daniel Carroll, both of Maryland, took opposite sides on the issue. Martin contended: "The Senate is to represent the states. Therefore, its members ought to be paid by the states."

"Not so," replied Carroll. "The Senate is to represent and manage the affairs of the whole nation, and should not advocate state interests. Therefore, Senators must not be made dependent on or paid by the states."

James Madison agreed, adding, "When states from the West are admitted, they will at first be too poor to support their senators."

Despite the brief flurry of disagreement, the delegates voted favorably on the Committee's recommendation that the national treasury assume the burden of all legislators' salaries.

On the matter of special requirements as to religion, residence, and property for those who wished to serve in Congress, the Committee of Detail had looked to the state constitutions. They found that all thirteen states had included property and residential qualifications in their constitutions. Two states, Virginia and New York, had no religious requirements for state representatives. The other eleven, strongly influenced in most matters by the Declaration of Independence, conceded that all men might have been created equal but they still intended to refuse to allow Catholics, Jews, and even some Protestants to serve in their state legislatures.

Avoiding the troublesome issue, the Committee of Detail made no recommendation on religious tests for office. But the youthful delegate from South Carolina, Charles Pinckney, forced a Convention decision by undertaking a one-man campaign to abolish such tests. Connecticut's Judge Roger Sherman was sure that no provision prohibiting a religious qualification was necessary. "Everyone," he insisted, "just took this prohibition for granted."

However, Pinckney succeeded in obtaining unanimous approval of wording to be added to the Constitution: "No religious test shall ever be required as a qualification to any office or public trust under the authority of the United States."

On the matter of a residential requirement there was no disagreement. Everyone felt that a member of Congress should be required to live in the state he represented in the national legislature. Nothing short of this would satisfy the states. And as a practical matter, this was the only way to provide meaningful representation.

But the Convention reversed the Committee of Detail recommendation on property, with the considerable help of Benjamin Franklin, who argued that limiting membership in Congress to property owners would be unfair to the common people. "There was no property qualification for fighting in the Revolution. Why should there be one now for serving in the government? Property owners have only one interest—increasing their own wealth and thus their own power. Besides, Europe will pay close attention to our new Constitution. If we seem to favor the rich, the most intelligent and enlightened men there will lose all respect for us. And common people will be discouraged about moving to this country."

Thus, qualifications turned out to be quite easily met. Even women were not specifically barred from trying for office. The Senate was to be the smaller legislative chamber, and slightly more selective: at least thirty years of age, nine years a United States citizen (this barred slaves and Indians), and a resident of the state to be represented. Term of office: six years.

Requirements for serving in the House of Representatives were ever so slightly scaled down: at least twenty-five years of age, seven years a United States citizen, and a resident of the state to be represented. Term of office: two years.

Qualifications as to who would be allowed to vote for national officers remained with the states.

Turning now to the Committee of Detail's recommendations on the specific powers granted to Congress, the delegates reopened the old question of where money bills should originate. In the spirit of compromise—and impatience to finish the business at hand and go home—they agreed that these bills would originate in the people's House of Representatives. However, they gave the Senate the right to submit changes, and stipulated that a majority of each house would have to vote final approval.

In listing the newly added powers of Congress, the Convention continued to de-emphasize the role of the states. Thus, they took away from the states the right to coin money. The states had no resources or credit in back of such money, and hence rampant inflation had been the result. In effect, the states were circulating what amounted to play money.

This was an easy power to take away from the states because the bad results had been so obvious and universal. Not so easy was the substitution of a national standing army for state militias, to be used to defend the nation and keep the peace. States' righters, such as Elbridge Gerry of Massachusetts and Luther Martin of Maryland, expressed deep fears that a national standing army would mean the end of freedom in the United States.

Gerry and his friends were outvoted on this motion, perhaps because they had just won another victory. They convinced the delegates that a declaration of war should be

made only on a vote of both houses of Congress, so that both the people and the states would have some voice in the decision. Wealthy Pierce Butler of South Carolina and others with his aristocratic leanings had argued unsuccessfully that the new President ought to have this power exclusively, just as the king had in all other countries.

In a further effort to calm fears of states' righters, the Convention voted to give Congress strict control over the military. They accomplished this by providing that no money should be appropriated for a period longer than two years.

Seeing tremendous changes in the country since the Declaration of Independence only eleven years previously, the delegates gave Congress a broad and flexible power to be used for all needs at all times: "To make all laws which shall be necessary and proper for carrying into execution the foregoing powers, and all other powers vested by this Constitution in the Government of the United States, or in any department or officer thereof." This section for obvious reasons soon won the nickname "the Elastic Clause."

At first glance this power seemed to undermine all the Convention's careful work to prevent tyranny by listing Congressional powers in detail. But here the delegates used the fact of two houses of Congress to make each serve as a check on tyrannical legislation by the other. They stipulated that legislation must be approved by both the House of Representatives and the Senate. And then under the doctrine of separation of powers into legislative, executive, and judicial branches, they provided that such legislation would then go to the President for his approval.

The Committee of Detail had gone far in submitting specific suggestions to improve the proposed new first article of the Constitution, covering the legislative branch. Now the members of the Convention themselves felt a sense of great satisfaction in further perfecting this Article, while successfully avoiding the twin extremes of anarchy and tyranny. Next the delegates turned their attention to the Committee's work on the second and third articles of the Constitution, dealing with the executive and judicial branches.

CHAPTER FIFTEEN

CHAIRMAN Nathaniel Gorham of the Convention's Committee of the Whole had written to the king of Prussia just a year ago, beseeching him to become king of the United States. Now, however, there was not the slightest doubt at the Convention that George Washington would become the first *President* of the United States. And he would be great. And he would always have the nation's best interests firmly in mind.

But who would follow him?

The gnawing doubts and fears brought on by this question made the arguments over how to elect a President continue until almost the last week of the Convention.

Time and again the delegates turned to lesser questions about the Presidency, because agreement here was so much easier. Thus, they approved the Committee of Detail recommendation that the President—and Vice President—be a minimum of thirty-five years old, superior (in age at least) to members of the House of Representatives by ten years and to senators by five years. Also, both men should have been born in the United States, or at least ought to be a citizen at the time of the adoption of the Constitution.

Some of the President's most important duties, the Committee proposed and the Convention agreed, must be shared with Congress, to prevent either from becoming all-powerful. Therefore, they had given Congress the power to declare war and to appropriate money for the armed forces. Now they specified the President as Commander in Chief of the Army and Navy and gave him the privilege of recommending whatever legislation or appropriations he found essential or desirable.

Treaties with foreign nations were to be made by and with the "advice and consent" of two thirds of the Senate present. The President could appoint ambassadors, judges, and other high government officials—but again only with the "advice and consent" of the Senate.

Why the Senate? Because it represented the states, which under the old Articles of Confederation had exercised these powers. However, James Wilson of Pennsylvania, both as member of the Committee of Detail and as spokesman for the large states, demanded that the House of Representatives also participate. "Giving this power to the Senate alone will mean the establishment of a dangerous aristocracy." But he was outvoted. Several delegates reminded doubters that the President, after all, was merely a glorified governor— of all thirteen states rather than of just one. More powerful, but to be cut from the same cloth.

Congress had the power to provide for calling forth the militia to execute the laws of the Union." The President was given responsibility "to take care that the laws be faithfully executed."

In the best of all possible countries, Congress and the President would work in a spirit of perfect harmony and cooperation. But just in case they did not, the Convention gave Congress the right to impeach the President. And it gave the President the right to veto laws passed by Congress.

But in neither case were these powers absolute. The delegates took care to prevent tyranny of any kind—by either house of Congress, by the President, or even tyranny by a majority.

Thus, each branch of Congress would have its own distinct role to play in impeachment proceedings. The House of Representatives would have to vote to impeach the President. The Senate would have to vote by two thirds of those present, with the chief justice of the Supreme Court in a presiding role, to convict and thus remove the President from office. By requiring a vote of two thirds for positive action, the Convention in effect gave to the one-third minority the power to prevent action.

The veto was a clever safeguard against tyrannical—or just plain poor—legislation. And here the delegates built in safeguards to prevent abuse of the safeguard. Hence the President might refuse to sign into law a piece of legislation passed by Congress. Each house of Congress had the power to override the President's veto if it could muster a vote of two thirds of those present. Again the President and one third of Congress—a distinct minority—could team up against the majority.

If the minority of members in Congress got out of hand they could be taken care of by not having their term of office renewed. But what about the President? And this brought the Convention back to that terrible dilemma—the fairest way to choose a President and whether to allow re-election. All the arguments for and against more than one term, for and against the various methods of election, were repeated endlessly.

The Committee of Detail had had no success in coming up with an acceptable compromise. Now, to deal with this one issue, the Convention set up the explicitly named Committee on Postponed Matters, with one representative from each of the eleven states currently participating. Judge David Brearley of New Jersey was chosen chairman of this group, which included some of the most famous and respected delegates: Nicholas Gilman of New Hampshire, Rufus King of Massachusetts, Judge Roger Sherman of Connecticut, Gouverneur Morris of Pennsylvania, John Dickinson of Delaware, Daniel Carroll of Maryland, James Madison of Virginia, Hugh Williamson of North Carolina, Pierce Butler of South Carolina, and Abraham Baldwin of Georgia.

Like the Great Compromise that had set up the formula for representation in the two houses of Congress, this issue demanded special treatment. The new Committee report, additional heated debate on the part of the entire Convention—plus impatience, exhaustion, and a haunting fear of failure—all conspired to bring about agreement.

States would play the key role in the election of the President to a four-year term, with no restriction as to re-election. Each state would have the privilege of choosing electors, equal to the number of representatives and senators of that state in Congress. In the event of a tie vote, the House of Representatives would choose one man from among those having the five highest totals. Each state in this procedure would have one vote. The delegates congratulated each other on preventing the painful confusion of a thirteen-way tie. At the same time they made it extraordinarily difficult, if not impossible, for a single state to provide both the President and the Vice President: "The electors shall meet in their respective states, and vote by ballot for two persons, of whom one at least shall not be an inhabitant of the same state with themselves."

For the Vice President the Convention showed little concern or respect. His one and only function would be to take over the office of President in an emergency. But in its report the Committee on Postponed Matters pointed out that if the Senate's presiding officer was to be chosen from the Senate itself, this would in effect deprive his home state of one representative. Therefore, they recommended one regular duty for the Vice President—presiding over the Senate and actually casting a vote in the event of a tie.

Elbridge Gerry of Massachusetts heatedly objected. "We might as well put the President himself at the head of the Senate. The close intimacy between the President and Vice President makes this function absolutely improper."

Gerry made no impression at all on the delegates. Even his own state voted to support the Committee.

Clearly there would be no monarch, not even a limited monarch, as head of the United States. Most of the delegates would live long enough to see whether this completely different kind of executive could and would succeed. Almost no one would live long enough to see the idea widely imitated.

CHAPTER SIXTEEN

BENJAMIN FRANKLIN could always be counted on for comic relief at even the most tense moments. And so it was that one day after a full session of squabbling over the report of the Committee of Detail, he announced his latest invention—a mangle to get rid of wrinkles in freshly washed clothes.

Leaving the hall that day, several delegates insisted that this was no invention. It could only be Benjamin Franklin's symbol for straightening out the wrinkles in the Convention.

"You are quite mistaken," George Washington said without the trace of a smile—so as not to expose his unattractive wooden false teeth. "I have seen the mangle and it works very well."

But symbol or not, the delegates worked harder that last month and could finally feel pride in their accomplishments. They had eagerly accepted John Rutledge's motion that they extend their hours of meeting by adjourning at 4 P.M., but "not one minute earlier."

No one disputed ex-Governor Rutledge of South Carolina when he asserted in his usual rapid-fire manner: "The public is becoming impatient. Besides, several members have already left the Convention for good. Our delegation has been here for every meeting and would like to finish the business at hand and go home."

Working on the judiciary turned out to be child's play compared to working on the legislative and executive branches. Even so, the judiciary would share equal importance with the other two branches. Thus the delegates felt compelled to give this third branch enormous power, not merely the leftover crumbs from the other branches.

The New Jersey Plan, Luther Martin of Maryand, and finally the Committee of Detail had all combined to produce the "Supreme Law of the Land" clause, which gave the judiciary power well beyond the six paragraphs allotted to this branch in the Constitution.

The words were few but packed with power: "This Constitution and the Laws of the United States which shall be made in Pursuance thereof, and all Treaties made or which shall be made, under the Authority of the United States, shall be the Supreme Law of the Land, and the Judges in every State shall be bound thereby, any Thing in the Constitution or Laws of any State to the Contrary notwithstanding."

What was the meaning of this paragraph, with all its carefully capitalized nouns? Simply—and explicitly—it meant that the national government was to be supreme, that any laws passed by the states in opposition to the national government were to be thrown out. Any laws passed by the national government, acting under the Constitution, were to be enforced by the national courts.

Surprisingly, the final straw that broke for all time the power of the states caused little argument. The national courts—not Congress, and certainly not the state courts— would have the authority to throw out state legislation found to be harmful to "national peace and harmony." In addition, the Supreme Court received the awesome power to settle disputes between states, or between a state and the national government.

Probably the greatest single criticism of the Articles of Confederation had been that Congress was unable to enforce legislation. Under the new Constiution, however, the United States was no longer to be an alliance of states bound by a treaty—in this case the Articles of Confederation. Rather, it was to be a nation bound by a law—the Constitution or "Supreme Law of the Land."

In extreme circumstances, armed might could be used to

support the law. But always, whether in extreme or ordinary circumstances, the law would be upheld and enforced by the national courts.

The one difficult point in establishing the judiciary branch—a point which again caused angry exchanges between large and small states—was the role of the state courts in a national court system. Several delegates insisted that the state courts should hear cases first, and the national courts should have jurisdiction only on appeal.

Again the delegates resorted to compromise. State courts were neither abolished nor made powerless. Instead, Congress was *permitted*, not required, to establish lower national courts. Both these lower national courts and the state courts could then exist side by side, each with carefully defined areas of authority.

From the beginning any hostess in the nation's capital who knew her etiquette—and national politics—unhesitatingly seated Supreme Court justices in special places of honor at her dinner parties. The Convention did not specifically tell the Supreme Court that it should have the overwhelming power to pass on the constitutionality of all Congressional legislation, that it could go so far as to declare legislation null and void if deemed in opposition to the Constitution.

But all of the Convention leaders assumed the existence of this power—James Wilson and Gouverneur Morris of Pennsylvania, Rufus King and Elbridge Gerry of Massachusetts, James Madison and George Mason of Virginia, and even one representative from a small state, Luther Martin of Maryland.

James Madison best summed up this point of view. "I

consider the difference between a system founded on the legislatures only and one founded on the people to be the true difference between a *league* or *treaty*, and a *Constitution*. A law violating a Constitution established by the representatives of the people themselves should be considered by the judges as null and void."

If the capital hostess was still not convinced of the im-

Livingston

Dickenson

Jefferson

Gouverneur
Morris

portance of the justices, somebody might remind her that national judges received the longest appointment of any government official: "Life on good behavior." Furthermore, judges could not be fired by the President—with or without the consent of the Senate. John Dickinson of Delaware, Elbridge Gerry of Massachusetts, and Roger Sherman of Connecticut had urged this power for the President —but unsuccessfully.

A judge who had been accused of committing a crime would lose his position if impeached by the House and convicted by the Senate. But he could never be dismissed for an unpopular decision. The delegates recalled with horror the colonial experience when judges were forced to decide cases not according to merit but according to the wishes of those in high office.

And as if all this power were not enough, the Convention deliberately took from Congress and gave to the judiciary the authority to decide what constituted treason. Once again the delegates felt warned by colonial experience to balance carefully the power of government and the liberty of the individual. Traitors attempting to destroy the country must be punished, they agreed, but without destroying the liberty of innocent persons.

Their solution was a very precise definition of treason: waging war against the United States or giving aid and comfort to its enemies. Furthermore, there would be no court conviction unless two witnesses testified to seeing the treasonous act being committed or unless the accused person confessed in open court.

By thus making treason convictions so difficult, the Convention showed its greater concern for protecting individual liberty. Too fresh in memory was the colonial experience where accusation of treason was used against any forward-looking person or any person even daring to disagree with the British government.

John Dickinson of Delaware put the matter well: "Experience must be our only guide. Reason may mislead us."

CHAPTER SEVENTEEN

THE COMMITTEE of Detail certainly had not neglected the states in its report. It cut them down in power—to perhaps one quarter of their importance under the Confederation—by making them just one more part of the country's government, along with the national legislative, executive, and judiciary branches.

No longer would the states be allowed to have their own armed forces—except for militias, even though these had been quite ineffective in keeping order. Instead, the national government would guarantee each state a republican form of government and would assume the responsiblity of protecting all citizens from foreign invasion and local disturbances. Here the Convention handled the states' sensitivities very gingerly. In the event of local disturbances the national government would send troops *only upon formal request of a state legislature.*

As a further protection for states, no new state was to be carved out of an already existing state or be created by joining together two or more neighboring states "without the consent of the Legislatures of the States concerned as well as of the Congress."

Again, like good parents, the delegates said no in equally firm terms to both the national and state governments. Neither would ever be permitted to reward citizens by granting titles of nobility. No dukes and duchesses, counts and countesses, lords and ladies.

Delegates made little objection to restrictions on state power. Why? Because these restrictions were taken almost word for word from the Articles of Confederation. Members of the Convention were used to the existence of such restrictions. The new dimension would be enforcement by the national courts and, if necessary, by armed might.

Nor did anyone—Northerner or Southerner—object to the clause granting the citizens of one state all rights and privileges of any other state. Never for a moment did the delegates discuss the possibility that one state's citizens might prove unacceptable to another state. Granting the rights and privileges of citizenship had been left to the states, not to the national government, with the result that Northern states, if they wished, could allow citizenship to free blacks living within their borders. In 1787 nobody raised the question of what might happen if these free blacks entered any Southern state: could they expect to retain their Northern-state citizenship, or would they have the same status of noncitizenship as the small number of former slaves who, though freed, chose to remain in the South?

Members of the Convention could foresee more of a problem with escaping slaves than with free blacks. Therefore, without wasting time on debate, South Carolina slaveholder Pierce Butler persuaded his fellow delegates to insert a clause providing for the capture and return of any runaway slave. The formal language used was "person held to service or labour in one state . . . escaping to another shall be delivered up on claim of the party to whom such service or labour may be due." No need to use possibly embarrassing words like "slave" or "master." But North Carolina, South Carolina, and Georgia made it very clear that only the inclusion of such a clause would ensure ratification by their legislatures. After all, they contended, it would make no sense to count three fifths of the slaves for representation and taxation, as the Convention had already agreed to do, if escape from the home state were allowed to go unhindered.

When it came to the slave trade, the South had to overcome considerable resistance. Speaking for South Carolina, wealthy and aristocratic General Charles Cotesworth Pinckney declared firmly: "Even if all my colleagues and I were to sign the Constitution and use all our personal influence, we could not get our state to agree to this Constitution if we take away the right of the states to import slaves. If you wish, put an import duty on slaves just as on other imports. But forbid the slave trade and you will exclude South Carolina from the Union."

John Dickinson, who had served as governor of both Pennsylvania and Delaware, could not take seriously this new threat of the three Southern states not to join the Union. "The real question ought to be whether the national happiness would be helped or hindered by importing slaves. Since the question involves the entire country, the decision ought to be left to the national government and not to the states particularly interested. Remember that Greece and Rome were made unhappy by their slaves."

George Mason of Virginia objected to encouraging slavery further by permitting the slave trade. "Slavery will prevent the immigration of whites who really enrich and strengthen a country. Every master of slaves is born a petty tyrant."

Dr. Hugh Williamson of North Carolina had a ready answer. "North Carolina has a constitution which permits the importation of slaves. The Southern states could not be members of the Union if the clause retaining importation of slaves is rejected. The South depends on agriculture and therefore depends completely on slaves. I strongly believe that it is wrong to force a state to agree to anything which is not absolutely necessary and which that state must refuse for its own well-being."

At this point John Rutledge of South Carolina came to the support of his fellow Southerners by making a formal motion to the effect that the slave trade be continued. And he added, in an effort to overcome Northern objections, that slaves should be taxed like any imports of property.

But strong opposition continued. Judge Roger Sherman of Connecticut emphasized his dislike of a tax on imported slaves because he could not accept the idea that they were *property*.

Governor Edmund Randolph of Virginia revealed the division between the states of the upper South and those of the lower South. "I would rather risk the Constitution than vote for Mr. Rutledge's motion. If we agree to this motion, we will revolt many citizens in states having no slaves. If we do not agree, two or three states might be lost to the

Union. Under the circumstances, I suggest we refer the matter to another committee for compromise."

The Convention agreed and at the same time gave the Committee the question of approving passage of Navigation Acts. Several delegates could hardly believe that the Convention was seriously considering Navigation Acts, restrictive laws like those that had been a chief cause of the Revolution for independence from England.

But now, borrowing heavily from English ideas and law, the North favored restricting shipment of all goods to United States-built vessels. This would increase immensely the North's commerce and shipbuilding industry.

The South wanted free trade for its raw materials with the outside world and therefore wanted to make passage of a restrictive Navigation Act difficult, if not impossible. John Rutledge of South Carolina and Edmund Randolph of Virginia, the two Southerners on the Committee of Detail, had included in that Committee's report a requirement that Navigation Acts would be passed only by a two-thirds vote of both houses of Congress.

Instant compromise was the order of the day, and so this latest of special committees made its report quickly. Members gave something to each section. For the North a majority vote of both Houses (and the North would have the majority of representatives in both Houses) would be sufficient to pass a Navigation Act. For the South the tax on importing slaves would be limited to ten dollars "for each person." To set the duty higher, it was agreed, would be using the power to tax in order to stop importation of slaves.

Out of consideration for both North and South, the Committee agreed to allow importing of slaves, but to set a time limit on this trade. The Committee suggested the year 1800 as the cutoff date. The Convention, threatened by the defection of the deep South, allowed itself to be convinced to extend the date to 1808.

James Madison was able to persuade his own state of Virginia—plus New Jersey, Pennsylvania, and Delaware— to vote against the extension. "So long a term will be more dishonorable to the national character," he declared with feeling, "than to say nothing about it in the Constitution." But the other seven states voted favorably, and the clause became part of the Constitution.

Gouverneur Morris of Pennsylvania tried one last time to show disapproval by changing the wording to specify "importation of slaves into North Carolina, South Carolina, and Georgia." However, George Mason of Virginia and Dr. Hugh Williamson of North Carolina convinced Morris to withdraw his motion "lest it should give offence to the people of these states."

Gouverneur Morris had not had much success as a statesman in this instance. Now in the midst of all the tension Alexander Hamilton appealed to his mischief-making instincts. Hamilton dared him to slap George Washington soundly on the back at dinner while inquiring, "And how are you today, my dear General? Morris accepted the challenge and the promise of dinner that went with it. Afterward, describing the ice-cold reaction from Washington, he shuddered, "Not for all the free dinners in the world would I ever try that again!"

CHAPTER EIGHTEEN

A MASTER stroke! In one fell swoop the delegates gave the country a way to correct all the Convention's mistakes and omissions—and gave a great boost to states' rights.

They did all this in a one-sentence paragraph providing for future amendments to the Constitution. Of course, the sentence was long—one hundred and thirty-nine words—and each word was carefully chosen and loaded with meaning.

On the subject of amending the Constitution the delegates never faltered in their thinking that the people should have the right to make changes in their Constitution. But when it came to specific procedures, the inevitable disagreements set in. Exactly what should be the role of the different branches of government, of the states, of the people?

The Committee of Detail had been too vague on the subject: "On the application of the Legislatures of two thirds of the States in the Union, for an amendment to this Constitution, the Legislature of the United States shall call a convention for that purpose."

At this critical juncture in the debate on a practical amending clause, the Convention heard from Alexander Hamilton, that strong nationalist who had recently returned to Philadelphia. He lost no time in mounting a floor fight to include Congress in the amending procedure.

He reminded the Convention that it had been almost impossible to amend the Articles of Confederation, and he denounced the Committee proposal. "State legislatures will not apply for changes except with a view to increase their own powers. The national legislature will be the first to realize the need for amendments. Therefore, I move that in addition to giving two thirds of the states the power to call a Constitutional Convention, the power also be given to Congress whenever two thirds of each House agree to call a Convention."

Then irony of ironies. To cap his argument, Hamilton, the convinced aristocrat, asserted, "There could be no danger in giving this power, as the people would make the final decision."

Once again the argument came down to a struggle between states' rights and a powerful national legislature. Now James Madison came up with the winning compromise: "Amendments to the Constitution should be proposed either by two thirds of both Houses or by the legislatures of two thirds of the states and then be ratified by three fourths of the state legislatures.

"There would be no need for Presidential approval as in the case of ordinary legislation. Nor could the courts declare a constitutional amendment unconstitutional as they could ordinary legislation. In changing the Constitution, the Congress and the states would be all-important."

But still the proposal remained stalled. Again the slavery issue intruded. Again North and South Carolina and Georgia felt threatened.

In ringing tones ex-Governor John Rutledge of South Carolina proclaimed: "I could never agree to give a power which would allow some states to change articles in the Constitution relating to slavery, even though these states had no interests in slavery and were indeed prejudiced against it. I propose that we add a proviso to ensure that no amendment interfere with the slave trade prior to the year 1808."

And so, with only Delaware dissenting, the amending clause was itself amended to this effect and passed.

That last month proved to be a good one for the states. Having been cut down in power for three months, they again found themselves being catered to. In addition to their new and major role in amending the Constitution, they were given a special proviso for their protection: "No state, without its consent, shall be deprived of its equal suffrage in the Senate."

They had Judge Roger Sherman of Connecticut to thank for this. Tall and awkward in his movements but a man of strong convictions, he frightened all the small states—and some of the large ones too—by picturing a conspiracy whereby three fourths of all the states might get together to abolish certain states or to deprive them of their equality in the Senate.

James Madison saw no sense in adding this particular proviso. "Begin with these special provisos and every state will insist on them for their boundaries, exports, and so on."

At first, with only Connecticut voting in favor, Sherman's proposal was roundly defeated. But the judge retaliated by moving to strike out the entire clause providing for amendments to the Constitution. Thus threatened, the Convention, with Gouverneur Morris acting as spokesman, came up with essentially the same proviso and passed it unanimously.

As James Madison wrote somewhat grouchily in his Convention diary that night, "This motion being dictated by the circulating murmurs of the small states was agreed to without debate, no one opposing it, or on the question, saying no."

CHAPTER NINETEEN

Concise wording and good organization. These were the watchwords of the framers of the Constitution. But like many great thinkers and writers they found that everything went topsy-turvy at the end. Result: the preamble—that glorious introduction of rolling phrases—was written and submitted the very last week.

A month before, the Committee of Detail had included a very businesslike preamble to its draft of the Constitution. Very matter-of-factly, with no trace of poetry or lilting prose, they wrote:

> We the people of the States of New Hampshire, Massachusetts, Rhode-Island and Providence Plantations, Connecticut, New York, New Jersey, Pennsylvania, Delaware, Maryland, Virginia, North-Carolina, South-Carolina, and Georgia, do ordain, declare and establish the following Constitution for the Government of Ourselves and our Posterity.

But there was a practical objection to this wording. The delegates had agreed that the Constitution would go into effect as soon as nine states had ratified, and no one could know in advance exactly which states would vote to ratify the Constitution.

Now as the Convention was coming to an end, the delegates appointed one last committee, the Committee on Style and Arrangement, to put the finishing touches on the Constitution. The Committee consisted of five strong nationalists: William Samuel Johnson of Connecticut as chairman, Rufus King of Massachusetts, Alexander Hamilton of New York, Gouverneur Morris of Pennsylvania, and James Madison of Virginia.

Very quickly these men submitted a preamble that signaled their abiilty to combine practical considerations and lofty ideals:

> We the People of the United States, in Order to form a more perfect Union, establish Justice, insure domestic Tranquillity, provide for the common Defence, promote the general Welfare, and secure the Blessings of Liberty to ourselves and our Posterity, do ordain and establish this Constitution for the United States of America.

Gratefully, and without any dissent, the Convention accepted the preamble. Next they proceeded to spend three days comparing carefully each clause and article submitted by the Committee on Style—Governeur Morris, by common consent the most gifted writer, made the largest contribution—with the hodgepodge of previous reports of other committees and general Convention debates. Some delegates complained of trickery in the Committee's rewording and rearranging of the Constitution. But most delegates pronounced themselves quite satisfied and expressed great annoyance at those who complained about "petty details."

The Convention felt a desperate need to present the Constitution to the country with the unanimous support of all delegates. Thus, the majority were quite willing to give in to the minority on minor points, provided no great principle was at stake.

However, of the fifty-five men who had attended the Convention, thirteen had left before the work was completed. Some made quite clear their disapproval of the proceedings. Others had to attend to personal matters such as business or family illness. Colonel George Mason and Governor Edmund Randolph of Virginia and Elbridge Gerry of Massachusetts were three leading delegates who stayed to the bitter end, hoping to change the Constitution to their own liking.

Mason, author of Virginia's Declaration of Rights, demanded similar protection for the people against the tyranny of the national government. "It will take only a few additional hours of our time to write a national Bill of Rights. Except for a few references to the state, it could be copied almost word for word from the Virginia Constitution."

Roger Sherman of Connecticut protested in his best Yankee accent: "State Bills of Rights are not being repealed by this Constitution and are therefore quite sufficient for purposes of protecting the people."

Colonel Mason was still not convinced. "The laws of the United States are to be above state Bills of Rights. Conceivably, the national government could someday eliminate these state laws. The matter is too important to be left to future chance."

Elbridge Gerry of Massachusetts, feeling as strongly on

the subject of human rights as that July day in 1776 when he had signed the Declaration of Independence, made a formal motion to the effect that a Bill of Rights be added to the Constitution. Mason promptly seconded the motion, losing his emotional control as he proclaimed the absolute need to copy the Virginia Declaration of Rights into the United States Constitution. But the motion was turned down by a Convention too impatient and too fatigued to consider even two or three more hours of writing.

Now Governor Randolph spoke out, with all the tact at his command. "It is painful for me to have to differ with the Convention at the close of the great and awful subject of their labors. However, I feel it necessary to call attention to the indefinite and dangerous power given by the Constitution to Congress. Therefore, I move that we call another Convention that will then consider amendments to the present plan which might be offered to the states."

Then he added, "I must warn you that if this proposal is disregarded, it will be impossible for me to sign the Constitution."

Mason quickly seconded Randolph's motion and Gerry joined in with a further objection—to the provision for representation of three fifths of the slaves.

Young Charles Pinckney of South Carolina took it upon himself to answer these three dissenters. "These declarations from members so respectable at the close of this important Convention make the present moment particularly solemn. However, I foresee nothing but confusion and disharmony if we should plan for a second Convention. I myself have many objections to the Constitution as it now stands. But I prefer to support the present plan rather than

to risk general confusion and the necessity of making decisions by armed might."

Randolph's proposal was unanimously voted down. Thereupon Randolph, Mason, and Gerry left the Convention permanently.

On the question of whether to agree to the Constitution as it now stood, all states voted aye. This suggested to Gouverneur Morris of Pennsylvania a way of making approval seem unanimous to the general public, while hiding the fact that of the original fifty-five delegates three men absolutely refused to sign and thirteen others had long since departed.

To give respectability to his idea, he persuaded Benjamin Franklin to propose that the Convention add these words to the end of the document: "Done in Convention by the unanimous consent of the *States* present the 17th of September . . . In Witness whereof we have hereunto subscribed our names."

The Convention approved the scheme eagerly. As each delegate walked to the front of the hall in order to sign his name, Benjamin Franklin broke the solemn silence. "I have often wondered whether that sun painted on the back of the President's chair was rising or setting. Now I have the happiness to know."

CHAPTER TWENTY

STILL NO REST for the weary delegates. They had fought long and hard in writing the Constitution. Now they had to take the fight to their own state ratifying conventions.

The Bill of Rights, which they had impatiently omitted from the Constitution for lack of time and energy, came to haunt them. The threat of several states to ignore the whole four months of proceedings in Philadelphia led to a firm promise that the new government would amend the Constitution to include a Bill of Rights.

But even this promise was not enough to satisfy the strong anti-Federalist faction in the nation which wanted power to remain with the states. An opinion poll in the country at the time would undoubtedly have revealed that the great majority of the public opposed strong central government as a new kind of tyranny and hence rejected the whole Constitution. Like Rhode Island, the public generally believed that the stronger the government, the greater the tyranny.

Three states finally ratified the Constitution in December of 1787—three months after the permanent adjournment of the Convention. Not surprisingly, two were tiny—Delaware and New Jersey, which hastened to signify approval before any large states changed their minds about equal votes in the Senate plus two extra Presidential electors for even the smallest states.

The third state to ratify in December was the second largest state in population, Pennsylvania, where the Federalists who supported strong national government deliberately hastened the proceedings before the anti-Federalists got a chance to organize. Even though the opposition was disorganized, they succeeded in winning to their side more than one third of the votes, so that the final tally was forty-three in favor to twenty-three opposed.

January of the new year saw two more states joining the list—the small state of Georgia unanimously, and Connecticut by a margin of better than three to one.

Then came Massachusetts, where opposition was running high. Rufus King and his Federalist friends undertook a personal campaign to win over each opposing delegate. To the point of exhaustion they repeated the pledge to add a Bill of Rights immediately. They even promised John Hancock, a leading anti-Federalist and opponent of the Constitution, their support for Vice President in the new government—a promise they never bothered to keep—if only he would vote to ratify.

A defeat in Massachusetts could have been a disaster. This state had long been a leader in the colonial struggle against England. It had also been the scene of the first bloodshed of the Revolution—1770 in the Boston Massacre and then 1775 in the Battle of Lexington and Concord. For Massachusetts to vote against ratification could very well have started a chain reaction leading to the defeat of the Constitution.

By the uncomfortably close margin of one hundred and eighty-seven in favor to one hundred and sixty-eight opposed, on February 6, 1788, Massachusetts became the sixth state to ratify.

Three more states were needed. By ample margins Maryland ratified on April 28, 1788, and South Carolina on May 23, 1788.

New Hampshire was the next state to vote. Even with the prospect of making history by becoming the ninth state to ratify and thus putting the Constitution into effect, the margin was close—fifty-seven in favor to forty-six opposed.

But no matter how close the vote, New Hampshire had at last, on June 21, 1788, given the United States a new government. Now everyone looked to the four remaining former colonies. Technically their votes were not needed to put the Constitution into effect. In fact, however, everyone agreed that a new government would make no sense without their participation.

Hamilton in New York and Madison in Virginia worked feverishly to convince their state conventions to ratify— even going so far as to publish anonymous essays explaining the work of the Convention. They had on their side the prestige of George Washington and Benjamin Franklin. Washington remarked publicly, "There is more wickedness than ignorance in anti-Federalism."

The result was that one month apart—and again by uncomfortably close margins—both states joined the new government: Virginia on June 26, 1788, with eighty-nine in

favor to seventy-nine opposed; New York on July 26, with thirty ayes to twenty-seven noes.

Patrick Henry now did his country a second great service. Having lost the fight against ratification, he set the tone for the defeated minority: "I will be a peaceable citizen. My head and my heart shall be ready to retrieve the loss of liberty and remove the defects of the citizen in a constitutional way."

Well over a year later, on November 21, 1789—seven months after the inauguration of George Washington as the first President—the twelfth state, North Carolina, voted favorably for ratification, by the lopsided margin of one hundred and ninety-four in favor to seventy-seven opposed.

Now everyone wondered about stubborn little Rhode Island. Even with the promise of a Bill of Rights, which she had demanded as her price for considering ratification, she balked. Then on May 29, 1790, almost two and a half years after Delaware had become the first state to ratify, Rhode Island voted to join the Union, but by the smallest of margins, thirty-four to thirty-two.

Finally the work of "that assembly of demigods," as Thomas Jefferson called them, was finished. The language of the Constitution now became the law of all thirteen states.

EPILOGUE

EPILOGUE

Even with the ratification of the Constitution by all thirteen states and the unanimous election of George Washington as first President of the United States, many still considered the Convention's work unfinished.

Again Massachusetts assumed leadership, this time to carry out the promise of adding a Bill of Rights to the Constitution. Before George Washington assumed office, the state enlisted his powerful support, with the result that he hinted in his Inaugural Address that Congress should immediately propose the necessary amendments to the Constitution.

In response four members of Congress—Representative James Madison of Virginia, Senator Oliver Ellsworth of Connecticut, Representative Daniel Carroll of Maryland, and Senator William Paterson of New Jersey—undertook to draft a Bill of Rights in the form of amendments to the Constitution. These were then approved by Congress and submitted to the individual states for ratification.

The Bill of Rights is the name commonly given to the

first ten amendments to the Constitution. This name and a great deal of the language came from a similar document set forth in England exactly one hundred years earlier in 1689. Also influential was George Mason's 1776 Virginia Declaration of Rights. In general these first ten amendments sought to balance the liberty of the individual and the duties of the government.

Not at all satisfied, several anti-Federalists continued to denounce the Constitution and the Bill of Rights. They sneered so loudly and so publicly that it seemed they might be the first who could benefit from that part of the First Amendment that prohibited Congress from restricting freedom of speech, press, assembly, or petition. The other part of this key amendment prohibited Congress from setting up a government-supported church or interfering with freedom of worship.

Those who sneered were in a distinct minority, however. Even men who, like Thomas Jefferson, had raised questions about scrapping the Articles of Confederation in favor of the Constitution, endorsed the Bill of Rights. Jefferson saw these amendments as protecting the individual by giving the courts legal means to curb abuses of power.

Every man's home, as in the most admired part of English tradition, was to be his castle. The Fourth Amendment made invasion of privacy difficult, allowing intrusion only after issuance of a complete and complicated warrant "describing the place to be searched, and the persons or things to be seized."

Fear of a revival of medieval torture or a return to the tyranny of colonial days showed up in several amendments. Thus, trial for crime could occur only after indictment by a grand jury. No person was ever to be tried more than once for the same crime or forced to incriminate or testify against himself. Due process of law was guaranteed to every person, assuring that government would be based on law, not on the whims of one man. And fair compensation was guaranteed for any property taken by the state for any reason.

Also, trial by a jury of his peers was to be every man's right. Anyone accused of a crime was to have a speedy and public trial, to be informed of the charges against him, and to be assisted by a lawyer. Excessive bail was outlawed, as were "cruel and unusual punishments."

As the Founding Fathers had intended, changing or adding to the Constitution turned out to be a cumbersome process, but not impossible. Two years after being drafted, final ratification of the first ten amendments came with the favorable vote of Virginia on December 15, 1791.

Massachusetts had led the fight for a Bill of Rights, but she was among the last of the thirteen states to ratify—one hundred and fifty years later! When the one hundred and fiftieth anniversary of the Bill of Rights was about to be celebrated with great fanfare in 1941, three of the original thirteen states realized to their horror and embarrassment that they never had formally ratified. Massachusetts, Connecticut, and Georgia had somehow overlooked the whole matter. Their failure to act had not made any difference since the necessary ten states—three fourths of the states as prescribed in the Constitution—had acted favorably.

Members of all three state legislatures hastened to ratify immediately in time for anniversary celebrations, thus becoming participants in a footnote to history.

WHO WAS WHO
AT THE CONVENTION?

Sketches of the fifty-five delegates, listed by states in geographical order. Delegates who did not sign the completed Constitution are indicated by an asterisk.

NEW HAMPSHIRE

NICHOLAS GILMAN (1755–1814), thirty-two, lawyer, member of the national Congress for two terms. Served on the eleven-member Convention Committee on Postponed Matters to find acceptable compromise on method of electing the President of the United States.

JOHN LANGDON (1741–1819), forty-six, extremely wealthy merchant with considerable political experience as state president (governor), speaker of the New Hampshire House, and twice a delegate to the national Congress. When the state could not raise funds to send delegates to Philadelphia, he donated enough money to cover expenses for two men, one of whom perhaps predictably was himself.

ELBRIDGE GERRY* (1744–1814), forty-three, wealthy merchant, Harvard-educated. Served in the Massachusetts state legislature and the national Congress. Signed both the Declaration of Independence and the Articles of Confederation. He constantly opposed measures leading to an overly strong centralized government, and quit the Convention at the very end after failure of his proposal to include a Bill of Rights in the Constitution itself.

NATHANIEL GORHAM (1738–1796), forty-nine, wealthy merchant. Despite his lack of education—he had left school at the age of fifteen—he was an excellent debater. His political experience included the state legislature and the national Congress (in which he served first as member and then as presiding officer), and judge of the Middlesex Court of Common Pleas. In general, he supported a strong national government. He played an important procedural role in the Constitution, first as chairman of the Committee of the Whole and then as a member of the five-man Committee of Detail.

RUFUS KING (1755–1827), thirty-two, lawyer. Educated at Harvard College, he was first in his graduating class and an excellent speaker. His political experience included serving in the national Congress. At the Convention he supported the Virginia Plan for a strong national government and spoke out against further importation of slaves. He served on the eleven-man Committee on Postponed Matters, set up to find an acceptable way to choose a President.

CALEB STRONG* (1745–1819), forty-two, lawyer. Harvard-educated, he served as state senator for several years, but declined election to the national Congress, probably for reasons of weak eyesight. At the Convention he strongly supported equal votes in the Senate for all states, regardless of wealth or population. His reasons for leaving Philadelphia at the end of August are unclear; he claimed family illness, but others pointed to a disagreement with his own delegation.

CONNECTICUT

OLIVER ELLSWORTH* (1745–1807), forty-two, judge of the Connecticut Supreme Court, educated at Yale. His previous political experience included membership on the governor's council. At the Convention he sponsored the Connecticut Compromise together with his two fellow delegates, and served on the five-man Committee of Detail. Family matters forced him to leave the Convention permanently on August 23.

WILLIAM SAMUEL JOHNSON (1727–1819), fifty, lawyer. He ranked third in his class at Yale, a class of fifteen students. Previous political experience included service in the national Congress. At the Convention he was appointed chairman of the Committee of Style and Arrangement, charged with putting the final touches on the Constitution.

ROGER SHERMAN (1721–1793), fifty-six, lawyer. Self-educated, he was a dull but determined speaker who at the Convention opposed an overly strong central government. His previous political experience consisted of service in the national Congress and as a state judge. Always concerned with his country's well-being, he was proud of having signed the Declaration of Independence and the Articles of Confederation.

NEW YORK

ALEXANDER HAMILTON (1757–1804), thirty, lawyer, graduate of Columbia. Constantly outvoted by his two fellow delegates, he left the Convention in disgust toward the end of the first month, returning occasionally for a few days. In the end he signed the completed document. When present, he argued strongly as an aristocrat and nationalist. Together with James Madison and John Jay he authored the *Federalist Papers*, explaining the Constitution and urging its ratification.

JOHN LANSING, JR.* (1754–1829), thirty-three, lawyer. He had been a member of the New York State legislature and the national Congress and a mayor of Albany, New York. At the Convention he supported the New Jersey Plan, favored by the small states. Together with his fellow delegate Robert Yates he walked out of the Convention for good early in July.

ROBERT YATES* (1724–1796), sixty-three, judge of the New York State Supreme Court. At the Convention he joined fellow delegate John Lansing, Jr., in opposing a strong national government.

NEW JERSEY

DAVID BREARLEY (1745–1790), forty-two, judge of the New Jersey Supreme Court, attended Princeton. At the Convention he supported the New Jersey Plan and served as chairman of the eleven-man Committee on Postponed Matters to deal with the problem of how best to elect a President.

JONATHAN DAYTON (1760–1824), twenty-seven, lawyer, graduate of Princeton. He was the youngest member of the Convention. He supported the New Jersey Plan and payment of United States senators by the national treasury.

WILLIAM CHURCHILL HOUSTON * (1746–1788), forty-one, Princeton graduate, former professor of mathematics and natural philosophy, lawyer. His political experience included membership in the national Congress. Because of serious illness, he left the Convention less than two weeks after formal opening.

WILLIAM LIVINGSTON (1723–1790), sixty-four, Yale graduate, lawyer, regularly reelected governor of his state since the Revolution. He was so tall and thin that he was nicknamed the "whipping post." He supported the New Jersey Plan, but seldom participated in any debate.

WILLIAM PATERSON (1745–1806), forty-two, lawyer, Princeton graduate. He served as state attorney general. He acted as chief spokesman for the New Jersey Plan in the Convention.

PENNSYLVANIA

GEORGE CLYMER (1739–1813), forty-eight, lawyer, signer of the Declaration of Independence, member of the national Congress. He followed the Convention debates carefully, but seldom spoke himself.

THOMAS FITZSIMONS (1741–1811), forty-six, merchant,

member of the Pennsylvania Assembly and of the national Congress. He rarely spoke at the Convention.

BENJAMIN FRANKLIN (1706–1790), eighty-one, philosopher. He was the oldest member of the Convention. His fellow delegate William Pierce of Georgia spoke admiringly of his possessing "an activity of mind equal to a youth of twenty-five years of age." He had been active politically all his life; he had signed the Declaration of Independence, but not the Articles of Confederation since he was serving as American ambassador to Paris at the time. He supported a strong national government at the Convention.

JARED INGERSOLL (1749–1822), thirty-eight, Yale graduate, lawyer, member of the national Congress. He was overshadowed at the Convention by other members of his delegation.

THOMAS MIFFLIN (1744–1800), forty-three, merchant, member of the Pennsylvania Assembly and of the national Congress, where he had once served as presiding officer. He was listed officially as head of the Pennsylvania delegation, but in practice was completely overshadowed by its more famous members.

GOUVERNEUR MORRIS (1752–1816), thirty-five, lawyer, graduate of Columbia. An excellent speaker who had long been active politically first in his native New York and then in Philadelphia, he made more speeches at the Convention than any other delegate. As a member of Congress from New York he had signed the Articles of Confederation in 1778. Probably his most important work at the Convention was helping to formulate the exact language of the Constitution as a member of the Committee of Style and Arrangement.

ROBERT MORRIS (1734–1806), fifty-three, merchant. He served as superintendent of finances during the Revolutionary War, signed both the Declaration of Independence and the Articles of Confederation, and was a member of the national Congress. He was friend and host of George Washington in Philadelphia. He spoke at the Convention only to nominate Washington as President of the Convention, but voted with his delegation in support of a strong national government.

JAMES WILSON (1742–1798), forty-five, lawyer. A native of Scotland, he was educated at the University of St. Andrews and the University of Edinburgh. A signer of the Declaration of Independence eleven years after his arrival in America, he then turned to politics and served several times in the national Congress. His encyclopedic knowledge of history, government, and philosophy earned him the reputation of Convention intellectual along with James Madison. He served as a member of the Committee of Detail, and in Convention debate supported a strong national government based on the people themselves.

DELAWARE

RICHARD BASSETT (1745–1815), forty-two, lawyer. He served as senator in the state legislature. At the Convention he was very quiet.

GUNNING BEDFORD, JR. (1747–1812), forty, lawyer, Princeton graduate, attorney general of Delaware, and member of Congress. He supported the position of the small states, but was flexible enough to agree to vote in favor of the Connecticut Compromise.

Jacob Broom (1752–1810), thirty-five, surveyor, member of the state house of representatives. He spoke more often in private than in public during the Convention.

John Dickinson (1732–1808), fifty-five, lawyer. He was famous as author of *The Letters from a Farmer in Pennsylvania*, in which he condemned the Townshend Acts of 1767 and denied the right of Parliament to tax the American colonies. He served as chairman of the committee of Congress charged with writing the Articles of Confederation, and was president (governor) first of Delaware, then of Pennsylvania. In the Convention he always emphasized the rights of states and of individuals.

George Read (1733–1798), fifty-four, lawyer. Served as state attorney general, member of the Delaware legislature and of the national Congress, and signed the Declaration of Independence. Although he was appointed head of the Delaware delegation, he took second place in Convention proceedings to his fellow delegate John Dickinson. He feared equally the power of the large states and the anarchy of the Articles of Confederation.

MARYLAND

Daniel Carroll (1730–1796), fifty-seven, signer of Declaration of Independence and member of the national Congress. At the Convention he supported election of the President by electors chosen by the people of the states and opposed having the states pay senators.

Daniel of Saint Thomas Jenifer (1723–1790), sixty-four, served in the Maryland senate and the national Congress. Did not take a leading part in the Convention, but stayed to the end to sign.

LUTHER MARTIN* (1748–1826), thirty-nine, lawyer, Princeton graduate. He served as attorney general of Maryland. He left the Convention because of his opposition to setting up a strong national government.

JAMES McHENRY (1753–1816), thirty-four, physician, educated in Dublin, Ireland. He was active politically in the Maryland state senate and the national Congress. Unenthusiastic about parts of the Constitution, he nevertheless felt it far preferable to the existing Articles of Confederation.

JOHN FRANCIS MERCER* (1759–1820), twenty-eight, lawyer, graduate of William and Mary College. He was a member of the Virginia legislature and the national Congress before becoming a resident of Maryland in 1785. He left the Convention permanently on August 17 to express disapproval of the strong national government being set up.

VIRGINIA

JOHN BLAIR (1732–1800), fifty-five, lawyer, graduate of William and Mary College. He served as chief justice of the Virginia Court of Appeals. Although he took no part in Convention debate, he approved and signed the completed Constitution.

JAMES MADISON (1751–1836), thirty-six, lawyer, Princeton graduate. He had served in the national Congress, and was the prime mover and supreme intellectual at the Convention. After signing the Constitution he worked with John Jay and Alexander Hamilton in writing the *Federalist Papers*, explaining the Constitution and supporting ratification. Later, as a member of the national House of Representatives, he was chairman of the committee that wrote the first ten amendments to the Constitution, the Bill of Rights.

GEORGE MASON* (1725–1792), sixty-two, planter, colonel in the Revolutionary army. His proudest accomplishment was authorship of the Virginia Declaration of Rights, the predecessor of all states' Bills of Rights. When the Convention refused to include a Bill of Rights in the main body of the Constitution itself, Mason, despite the large and constructive role he had played in the framing of the Constitution, refused to sign.

JAMES McCLURG* (1746–1823), forty-one, physician. He had very little political experience and decided by mid-August to leave the Convention permanently, feeling that the Virginia delegation had no particular need of him.

EDMUND RANDOLPH* (1753–1813), thirty-four, lawyer, graduate of William and Mary College, governor of Virginia. He was one of the authors of and chief spokesman for the fifteen articles of the Virginia Plan, and he served on the Committee of Detail. Although he refused to sign the completed Constitution because of the failure to include a Bill of Rights, he later played a leading role in convincing the Virginia Ratification Convention to vote favorably.

GEORGE WASHINGTON (1732–1799), fifty-five, planter. He was universally considered the father of his country, and his presence alone seemed to predict a successful outcome for the Convention. Although he rarely spoke publicly during the sessions, his votes in the Virginia delegation were known to reflect the same strong nationalist views expressed by Madison.

GEORGE WYTHE* (1726–1806), sixty-one, professor of

law at William and Mary College. A signer of the Declaration of Independence, his main role at the Convention was chairman of the committee that drew up the rules under which the delegates operated. His wife's illness caused him to return home permanently some ten days after the official opening of the Convention. Despite his failure to sign the Constitution, he worked hard for a favorable vote at the Virginia Ratification Convention.

NORTH CAROLINA

WILLIAM BLOUNT (1749–1800), thirty-eight, merchant and Western land speculator. He served in the North Carolina state legislature and in the national Congress. He left the Convention on June 20 to attend the North Carolina Assembly, then proceeded to New York to attend Congress until August 3, at which point he remained at the Convention until the end. An inactive delegate.

WILLIAM RICHARDSON DAVIE* (1756–1820), thirty-one, lawyer, Princeton graduate, member of the North Carolina legislature. In the Convention he favored equal votes for each state in the Senate and the three-fifths ratio for representation of slaves in the House. Pressure of his legal practice made him decide to return home permanently on August 13.

ALEXANDER MARTIN* (1740–1807), forty-seven, politician, Princeton graduate. He had served as a member of the state senate and as governor. Although named head of his delegation, he was an inactive delegate and decided to leave Philadelphia permanently late in August, on the grounds that his continued presence would make no difference in the final outcome.

RICHARD DOBBS SPAIGHT (1758–1802), twenty-nine. Although born in North Carolina, he was educated at the University of Glasgow, Scotland. He served in the North Carolina legislature and in the national Congress. At the Convention he opposed equal votes for states in the Senate.

HUGH WILLIAMSON (1735–1819), fifty-two, physician, member of the first graduating class of the College of Philadelphia. Also studied abroad. He served in the state legislature and in the national Congress. At the Convention he was a member of the eleven-man Committee on Postponed Matters, created to find an acceptable compromise for a method of electing the President of the United States.

SOUTH CAROLINA

PIERCE BUTLER (1744–1822), forty-three, planter. He served in the South Carolina state legislature and in Congress. He heartily approved of the separation of powers into legislative, executive, and judicial branches, and also was responsible for the insertion into the Constitution itself of the Fugitive Slave clause.

CHARLES PINCKNEY (1757–1824), thirty, lawyer, member of the national Congress. He undertook a successful one-man campaign to have included in the Constitution a clause forbidding religious tests for office in the United States government.

CHARLES COTESWORTH PINCKNEY (1746–1825), forty-one, general in the Revolutionary army, lawyer, attended Christ Church College, Oxford, England. He served in the lower house of the South Carolina state legislature. He was the cousin of the younger Charles Pinckney. An effective supporter of strong national government, he was considered one of the key delegates at the Convention.

JOHN RUTLEDGE (1739–1800), forty-eight, lawyer, head of his state delegation. He served as governor of South Carolina and member of the general assembly of the state and of the national Congress. At the very beginning of the Convention he and Robert Morris escorted Washington to the front of the hall after Washington's election as President of the Convention. He was a member of the Committee of Detail and supported a strong national government.

GEORGIA

ABRAHAM BALDWIN (1754–1807), thirty-three, lawyer, Yale graduate. He served in the Georgia state legislature and the national Congress. Considered the ablest member of the Georgia delegation, he served on the committee set up to compromise the issues of representation and the origin of money bills.

WILLIAM FEW (1748–1828), thirty-nine, lawyer, just one year of formal education. He had read widely on his own in the fields of ancient and modern history, philosophy, and astronomy. He served in the Georgia legislature and the national Congress. Although he took no part in Convention debate, he was conscientious in attendance.

WILLIAM HOUSTOUN* (1757–1812), thirty, lawyer. He had been a member of the Georgia state legislature and of the national Congress. At the Convention he favored proportional representation in both houses of the national legislature. He remained in Philadelphia until the end of July, when he left for home for personal reasons.

WILLIAM PIERCE* (1740–1789), forty-seven, merchant. He had served in the national Congress. His contribution to the Convention was minor. He is noted for succinct character sketches of his fellow Convention delegates. Of his presence at the Convention, he wrote with good humor: "I possess ambition and it was that and the flattering opinion of some of my friends that gave me a seat in the wisest council in the world." He left the Convention on July 1 to attend the Congress of the Confederation meeting in New York. He indicated that had he been present on the final day in Philadelphia he would have signed the completed Constitution.

THE CONSTITUTION
OF THE UNITED STATES
OF AMERICA

WE, the People of the United States, in order to form a more perfect union, establish justice, insure domestic tranquility, provide for the common defence, promote the general welfare, and secure the blessings of liberty to ourselves and our posterity, do ordain and establish this Constitution for the United States of America.

ARTICLE I.

Sect. 1. A L L legislative powers herein granted shall be vested in a Congress of the United States, which shall consist of a Senate and House of Representatives.

Sect. 2. The House of Representatives shall be composed of members chosen every second year by the people of the several states, and the electors in each state shall have the qualifications requisite for electors of the most numerous branch of the state legislature.

No person shall be a representative who shall not have attained to the age of twenty-five years, and been seven years a citizen of the United States, and who shall not, when elected, be an inhabitant of that state in which he shall be chosen.

* [Representatives and direct taxes shall be apportioned among

* The part enclosed by brackets was changed by section 2 of Amend‑ ment XIV.

the several states which may be included within this Union, according to their respective numbers, which shall be determined by adding to the whole number of free persons, including those bound to service for a term of years, and excluding Indians not taxed, three-fifths of all other persons.] The actual enumeration shall be made within three years after the first meeting of the Congress of the United States, and within every subsequent term of ten years, in such manner as they shall by law direct. The number of representatives shall not exceed one for every thirty thousand, but each state shall have at least one representative; and until such enumeration shall be made, the state of New-Hampshire shall be entitled to chuse three, Massachusetts eight, Rhode-Island and Providence Plantations one, Connecticut five, New-York six, New-Jersey four, Pennsylvania eight, Delaware one, Maryland six, Virginia ten, North-Carolina five, South-Carolina five, and Georgia three.

When vacancies happen in the representation from any state, the Executive authority thereof shall issue writs of election to fill such vacancies.

The House of Representatives shall chuse their Speaker and other officers; and shall have the sole power of impeachment.

Sect. 3. The Senate of the United States shall be composed of two senators from each state, * [chosen by the legislature thereof,] for six years; and each senator shall have one vote.

Immediately after they shall be assembled in consequence of the first election, they shall be divided as equally as may be into three classes. The seats of the senators of the first class shall be vacated at the expiration of the second year, of the second class at the expiration of the fourth year, and of the third class at the expiration of the sixth year, so that one-third may be chosen every second year; † [and if vacancies happen by resignation, or otherwise, during the recess of the Legislature of any state, the Executive thereof may make temporary appointments until the next meeting of the Legislature, which shall then fill such vacancies.]

No person shall be a senator who shall not have attained to the age of thirty years, and been nine years a citizen of the United

* The clause enclosed by brackets was changed by clause 1 of Amendment XVII.

† The part enclosed by brackets was changed by clause 2 of Amendment XVII.

States, and who shall not, when elected, be an inhabitant of that state for which he shall be chosen.

The Vice-President of the United States shall be President of the senate, but shall have no vote, unless they be equally divided.

The Senate shall chuse their other officers, and also a President pro tempore, in the absence of the Vice-President, or when he shall exercise the office of President of the United States.

The Senate shall have the sole power to try all impeachments. When sitting for that purpose, they shall be on oath or affirmation. When the President of the United States is tried, the Chief Justice shall preside: And no person shall be convicted without the concurrence of two-thirds of the members present.

Judgment in cases of impeachment shall not extend further than to removal from office, and disqualification to hold and enjoy any office of honor, trust or profit under the United States; but the party convicted shall nevertheless be liable and subject to indictment, trial, judgment and punishment, according to law.

Sect. 4. The times, places and manner of holding elections for senators and representatives, shall be prescribed in each state by the legislature thereof; but the Congress may at any time by law make or alter such regulations, except as to the places of chusing Senators.

The Congress shall assemble at least once in every year, and such meeting shall * [be on the first Monday in December,] unless they shall by law appoint a different day.

Sect. 5. Each house shall be the judge of the elections, returns and qualifications of its own members, and a majority of each shall constitute a quorum to do business; but a smaller number may adjourn from day to day, and may be authorized to compel the attendance of absent members, in such manner, and under such penalties as each house may provide.

Each house may determine the rules of its proceedings, punish its members for disorderly behaviour, and, with the concurrence of two-thirds, expel a member.

Each house shall keep a journal of its proceedings, and from time to time publish the same, excepting such parts as may in their judgment require secrecy; and the yeas and nays of the members of

* The clause enclosed by brackets was changed by section 2 of Amendment XX.

either house on any question shall, at the desire of one-fifth of those present, be entered on the journal.

Neither house, during the session of Congress, shall, without the consent of the other, adjourn for more than three days, nor to any other place than that in which the two houses shall be sitting.

Sect. 6. The senators and representatives shall receive a compensation for their services, to be ascertained by law, and paid out of the treasury of the United States. They shall in all cases, except treason, felony and breach of the peace, be privileged from arrest during their attendance at the session of their respective houses, and in going to and returning from the same; and for any speech or debate in either house, they shall not be questioned in any other place.

No senator or representative shall, during the time for which he was elected, be appointed to any civil office under the authority of the United States, which shall have been created, or the emoluments whereof shall have been encreased during such time; and no person holding any office under the United States, shall be a member of either house during his continuance in office.

Sect. 7. All bills for raising revenue shall originate in the house of representatives; but the senate may propose or concur with amendments as on other bills.

Every bill which shall have passed the house of representatives and the senate, shall, before it become a law, be presented to the president of the United States; if he approve he shall sign it, but if not he shall return it, with his objections to that house in which it shall have originated, who shall enter the objections at large on their journal, and proceed to reconsider it. If after such reconsideration two-thirds of that house shall agree to pass the bill, it shall be sent, together with the objections, to the other house, by which it shall likewise be reconsidered, and if approved by two-thirds of that house, it shall become a law. But in all such cases the votes of both houses shall be determined by yeas and nays, and the names of the persons voting for and against the bill shall be entered on the journal of each house respectively. If any bill shall not be returned by the President within ten days (Sundays excepted) after it shall have been presented to him, the same shall be a law, in like manner as if he had signed it, unless the Congress by their adjournment prevent its return, in which case it shall not be a law.

Every order, resolution, or vote to which the concurrence of the Senate and House of Representatives may be necessary (except on a question of adjournment) shall be presented to the President of the United States; and before the same shall take effect, shall be approved by him, or, being disapproved by him, shall be repassed by two-thirds of the Senate and House of Representatives, according to the rules and limitations prescribed in the case of a bill.

Sect. 8. The Congress shall have power.

To lay and collect taxes, duties, imposts and excises, to pay the debts and provide for the common defence and general welfare of the United States; but all duties, imposts and excises shall be uniform throughout the United States;

To borrow money on the credit of the United States;

To regulate commerce with foreign nations, and among the several states, and with the Indian tribes;

To establish an uniform rule of naturalization, and uniform laws on the subject of bankruptcies throughout the United States;

To coin money, regulate the value thereof, and of foreign coin, and fix the standard of weights and measures;

To provide for the punishment of counterfeiting the securities and current coin of the United States;

To establish post offices and post roads;

To promote the progress of science and useful arts, by securing for limited times to authors and inventors the exclusive right to their respective writings and discoveries;

To constitute tribunals inferior to the supreme court;

To define and punish piracies and felonies committed on the high seas, and offences against the law of nations;

To declare war, grant letters of marque and reprisal, and make rules concerning captures on land and water;

To raise and support armies, but no appropriation of money to that use shall be for a longer term than two years;

To provide and maintain a navy;

To make rules for the government and regulation of the land and naval forces;

To provide for calling forth the militia to execute the laws of the union, suppress insurrections and repel invasions;

To provide for organizing, arming, and disciplining, the militia, and for governing such part of them as may be employed in the service of the United States, reserving to the States repectively, the appointment of the officers, and the authority of training the militia according to the discipline prescribed by Congress;

To exercise exclusive legislation in all cases whatsoever, over such district (not exceeding ten miles square) as may, by cession of particular States, and the acceptance of Congress, become the seat of the government of the United States, and to exercise like authority over all places purchased by the consent of the legislature of the state in which the same shall be, for the erection of forts, magazines, arsenals, dock-yards, and other needful buildings;—And

To make all laws which shall be necessary and proper for carrying into execution the foregoing powers, and all other powers vested by this constitution in the government of the United States, or in any department or officer thereof.

Sect. 9. The migration or importation of such persons as any of the states now existing shall think proper to admit, shall not be prohibited by the Congress prior to the year one thousand eight hundred and eight, but a tax or duty may be imposed on such importation, not exceeding ten dollars for each person.

The privilege of the writ of habeas corpus shall not be suspended, unless when in cases of rebellion or invasion the public safety may require it.

No bill of attainder or ex post facto law shall be passed.

No capitation, or other direct, tax shall be laid, unless in proportion to the census or enumeration herein before directed to be taken.*

No tax or duty shall be laid on articles exported from any state. No preference shall be given by any regulation of commerce or revenue to the ports of one state over those of another: nor shall vessels bound to, or from, one state, be obliged to enter, clear, or pay duties in another.

No money shall be drawn from the treasury, but in consequence of appropriations made by law; and a regular statement and account of the receipts and expenditures of all public money shall be published from time to time.

No title of nobility shall be granted by the United States:—And no person holding any office of profit or trust under them, shall, without the consent of the Congress, accept of any present, em-

* *See also* Amendment XVI.

olument, office, or title, of any kind whatever, from any king, prince, or foreign state.

Sect. 10. No state shall enter into any treaty, alliance, or confederation; grant letters of marque and reprisal; coin money; emit bills of credit; make any thing but gold and silver coin a tender in payment of debts; pass any bill of attainder, ex post facto law, or law impairing the obligation of contracts, or grant any title of nobility.

No state shall, without the consent of the Congress, lay any imposts or duties on imports or exports, except what may be absolutely necessary for executing its inspection laws; and the net produce of all duties and imposts, laid by any state on imports or exports, shall be for the use of the Treasury of the United States; and all such laws shall be subject to the revision and controul of the Congress. No state shall, without the consent of Congress, lay any duty of tonnage, keep troops, or ships of war in time of peace, enter into any agreement or compact with another state, or with a foreign power, or engage in war, unless actually invaded, or in such imminent danger as will not admit of delay.

II.

Sect. 1. The executive power shall be vested in a president of the United States of America. He shall hold his office during the term of four years, and, together with the vice-president, chosen for the same term, be elected as follows.

Each state shall appoint, in such manner as the legislature thereof may direct, a number of electors, equal to the whole number of senators and representatives to which the state may be entitled in the Congress: but no senator or representative, or person holding an office of trust or profit under the United States, shall be appointed an elector.

* [The electors shall meet in their respective states, and vote by ballot for two persons, of whom one at least shall not be an inhabitant of the same state with themselves. And they shall make a list of all the persons voted for, and of the number of votes for each; which list they shall sign and certify, and transmit sealed to the seat of the government of the United States, directed to the president of the senate. The president of the senate shall, in the

* This paragraph has been superseded by Amendment XII.

presence of the senate and house of representatives, open all the certificates, and the votes shall then be counted. The person having the greatest number of votes shall be the president, if such number be a majority of the whole number of electors appointed; and if there be more than one who have such majority, and have an equal number of votes, then the house of representatives shall immediately chuse by ballot one of them for president; and if no person have a majority, then from the five highest on the list the said house shall in like manner chuse the president. But in chusing the president, the votes shall be taken by states, the representation from each state having one vote; a quorum for this purpose shall consist of a member or members from two-thirds of the states, and a majority of all the states shall be necessary to a choice. In every case, after the choice of the president, the person having the greatest number of votes of the electors shall be the vice-president. But if there should remain two or more who have equal votes, the senate shall chuse from them by ballot the vice-president.]

The Congress may determine the time of chusing the electors, and the day on which they shall give their votes; which day shall be the same throughout the United States.

No person except a natural born citizen, or a citizen of the United States, at the time of the adoption of this constitution, shall be eligible to the office of president; neither shall any person be eligible to that office who shall not have attained to the age of thirty-five years, and been fourteen years a resident within the United States.

† In case of the removal of the president from office, or of his death, resignation, or inability to discharge the powers and duties of the said office, the same shall devolve on the vice-president, and the Congress may by law provide for the case of removal, death, resignation or inability, both of the president and vice-president, declaring what officer shall then act as president, and such officer shall act accordingly, until the disability be removed, or a president shall be elected.

The president shall, at stated times, receive for his services, a compensation, which shall neither be encreased nor diminished during the period for which he shall have been elected, and he shall

† This clause has been affected by Amendment XXV.

not receive within that period any other emolument from the United States, or any of them.

Before he enter on the execution of his office, he shall take the following oath or affirmation:

"I do solemnly swear (or affirm) that I will faithfully execute the office of president of the United States, and will to the best of my ability, preserve, protect and defend the constitution of the United States."

Sect. 2. The president shall be commander in chief of the army and navy of the United States, and of the militia of the several States, when called into the actual service of the United States; he may require the opinion, in writing, of the principal officer in each of the executive departments, upon any subject relating to the duties of their respective offices, and he shall have power to grant reprieves and pardons for offences against the United States, except in cases of impeachment.

He shall have power, by and with the advice and consent of the senate, to make treaties, provided two-thirds of the senators present concur; and he shall nominate, and by and with the advice and consent of the senate, shall appoint ambassadors, other public ministers and consuls, judges of the supreme court, and all other officers of the United States, whose appointments are not herein otherwise provided for, and which shall be established by law But the Congress may by law vest the appointment of such inferior officers, as they think proper, in the president alone, in the courts of law, or in the heads of departments.

The president shall have power to fill up all vacancies that may happen during the recess of the senate, by granting commissions which shall expire at the end of their next session.

Sect. 3. He shall from time to time give to the Congress information of the state of the union, and recommend to their consideration such measures as he shall judge necessary and expedient; he may, on extraordinary occasions, convene both houses, or either of them, and in case of disagreement between them, with respect to the time of adjournment, he may adjourn them to such time as he shall think proper; he shall receive ambassadors and other public ministers; he shall take care that the laws be faithfully executed, and shall commission all the officers of the United States.

Sect. 4. The president, vice-president and all civil officers of the

United States, shall be removed from office on impeachment for, and conviction of, treason, bribery, or other high crimes and misdemeanors.

III.

Sect. 1. The judicial power of the United States, shall be vested in one supreme court, and in such inferior courts as the Congress may from time to time ordain and establish. The judges, both of the supreme and inferior courts, shall hold their offices during good behaviour, and shall, at stated times, receive for their services, a compensation, which shall not be diminished during their continuance in office.

Sect. 2. The judicial power shall extend to all cases, in law and equity, arising under this constitution, the laws of the United States, and treaties made or which shall be made, under their authority; to all cases affecting ambassadors, other public ministers and consuls; to all cases of admiralty and maritime jurisdiction; to controversies to which the United States shall be a party; to controversies between two or more States, between a state and citizens of another state, * between citizens of different States, between citizens of the same state claiming lands under grants of different States, and between a state, or the citizens thereof, and foreign States, citizens or subjects.

In all cases affecting ambassadors, other public ministers and consuls, and those in which a state shall be party, the supreme court shall have original jurisdiction. In all the other cases before mentioned, the supreme court shall have appellate jurisdiction, both as to law and fact, with such exceptions, and under such regulations as the Congress shall make.

The trial of all crimes, except in cases of impeachment, shall be by jury; and such trial shall be held in the state where the said crimes shall have been committed; but when not committed within any state, the trial shall be at such place or places as the Congress may by law have directed.

Sect. 3. Treason against the United States, shall consist only in levying war against them, or in adhering to their enemies, giving them aid and comfort. No person shall be convicted of treason

*This clause has been affected by Amendment XI.

unless on the testimony of two witnesses to the same overt act, or on confession in open court.

The Congress shall have power to declare the punishment of treason, but no attainder of treason shall work corruption of blood, or forfeiture except during the life of the person attainted.

IV.

Sect. 1. Full faith and credit shall be given in each state to the public acts, records, and judicial proceedings of every other state. And the Congress may by general laws prescribe the manner in which such acts, records and proceedings shall be proved, and the effect thereof.

Sect. 2. The citizens of each state shall be entitled to all privileges and immunities of citizens in the several states.

A person charged in any state with treason, felony, or other crime, who shall flee from justice, and be found in another state, shall, on demand of the executive authority of the state from which he fled, be delivered up, to be removed to the state having jurisdiction of the crime.

* [No person held to service or labour in one state, under the laws thereof, escaping into another, shall, in consequence of any law or regulation therein, be discharged from such service or labour, but shall be delivered up on claim of the party to whom such service or labour may be due.]

Sect. 3. New states may be admitted by the Congress into this union; but no new state shall be formed or erected within the jurisdiction of any other state; nor any state be formed by the junction of two or more states, or parts of states, without the consent of the legislatures of the states concerned as well as of the Congress.

The Congress shall have power to dispose of and make all needful rules and regulations respecting the territory or other property belonging to the United States; and nothing in this Constitution shall be so construed as to prejudice any claims of the United States, or of any particular state.

Sect. 4. The United States shall guarantee to every state in this union a Republican form of government, and shall protect each of them against invasion; and on application of the legislature, or of

* This paragraph has been superseded by Amendment XIII.

the executive (when the legislature cannot be convened) against domestic violence.

V.

The Congress, whenever two-thirds of both houses shall deem it necessary, shall propose amendments to this constitution, or, on the application of the legislatures of two-thirds of the several states, shall call a convention for proposing amendments, which, in either case, shall be valid to all intents and purposes, as part of this constitution, when ratified by the legislatures of three-fourths of the several states, or by conventions in three-fourths thereof, as the one or the other mode of ratification may be proposed by the Congress; Provided, that no amendment which may be made prior to the year one thousand eight hundred and eight shall in any manner affect the first and fourth clauses in the ninth section of the first article; and that no state, without its consent, shall be deprived of its equal suffrage in the senate.

VI.

All debts contracted and engagements entered into, before the adoption of this Constitution, shall be as valid against the United States under this Constitution, as under the confederation.

This constitution, and the laws of the United States which shall be made in pursuance thereof; and all treaties made, or which shall be made, under the authority of the United States, shall be the supreme law of the land; and the judges in every state shall be bound thereby, any thing in the constitution or laws of any state to the contrary notwithstanding.

The senators and representatives beforementioned, and the members of the several state legislatures, and all executive and judicial officers, both of the United States and of the several States, shall be bound by oath or affirmation, to support this constitution; but no religious test shall ever be required as a qualification to any office or public trust under the United States.

VII.

The ratification of the conventions of nine States, shall be sufficient for the establishment of this constitution between the States so ratifying the same.

Done in Convention, by the unanimous consent of the States present, the seventeenth day of September, in the year of our Lord one thousand seven hundred and eighty-seven, and of the Independence of the United States of America the twelfth. In witness whereof we have hereunto subscribed our Names.*

GEORGE WASHINGTON, President, And Deputy from VIRGINIA.

NEW-HAMPSHIRE.	*John Langdon,* *Nicholas Gilman.*
MASSACHUSETTS.	*Nathaniel Gorham,* *Rufus King.*
CONNECTICUT.	*William Samuel Johnson,* *Roger Sherman.*
NEW-YORK.	*Alexander Hamilton.*
NEW-JERSEY.	*William Livingston,* *David Brearley,* *William Paterson,* *Jonathan Dayton.*
PENNSYLVANIA.	*Benjamin Franklin,* *Thomas Mifflin,* *Robert Morris,* *George Clymer,* *Thomas Fitzsimons,* *Jared Ingersoll,* *James Wilson,* *Gouverneur Morris.*
DELAWARE.	*George Read,* *Gunning Bedford, Junior,* *John Dickinson,* *Richard Bassett,* *Jacob Broom.*

* Braces and spelling of names conform to original printed copy. Capitalization of nouns and spelling of words throughout the document varied from one printer to another.

MARYLAND.	James M'Henry, Daniel of St. Tho. Jenifer, Daniel Carrol.
VIRGINIA.	John Blair, James Madison, Junior.
NORTH-CAROLINA.	William Blount, Richard Dobbs Spaight, Hugh Williamson.
SOUTH-CAROLINA.	John Rutledge, Charles Cotesworth Pinckney, Charles Pinckney, Pierce Butler.
GEORGIA.	William Few, Abraham Baldwin.

Attest, *William Jackson*, SECRETARY.

AMENDMENTS
TO THE CONSTITUTION

ARTICLES in addition to, and Amendment of the Constitution of *the United States of America, proposed by Congress, and ratified by the Legislatures of the several States, pursuant to the fifth Article of the original Constitution.*

ARTICLE [I]

Congress shall make no law respecting an establishment of religion, or prohibiting the free exercise thereof; or abridging the freedom of speech, or of the press; or the right of the people peaceably to assemble, and to petition the Government for a redress of grievances.

ARTICLE [II]

A well regulated Militia, being necessary to the security of a free State, the right of the people to keep and bear Arms, shall not be infringed.

ARTICLE [III]

No Soldier shall, in time of peace be quartered in any house, without the consent of the Owner, nor in time of war, but in a manner to be prescribed by law.

ARTICLE [IV]

The right of the people to be secure in their persons, houses, papers, and effects, against unreasonable searches and seizures, shall not be violated, and no Warrants shall issue, but upon probable cause, supported by Oath or affirmation, and particularly describing the place to be searched, and the persons or things to be seized.

ARTICLE [V]

No person shall be held to answer for a capital, or otherwise infamous crime, unless on a presentment or indictment of a Grand Jury, except in cases arising in the land or naval forces, or in the Militia, when in actual service in time of War or public danger; nor shall any person be subject for the same offence to be twice put in jeopardy of life or limb; nor shall be compelled in any criminal case to be a witness against himself, nor be deprived of life, liberty, or property, without due process of law; nor shall private property be taken for public use, without just compensation.

ARTICLE [VI]

In all criminal prosecutions, the accused shall enjoy the right to a speedy and public trial, by an impartial jury of the State and district wherein the crime shall have been committed, which district shall have been previously ascertained by law, and to be informed of the nature and cause of the accusation; to be confronted with the witnesses against him; to have compulsory process for obtaining witnesses in his favor, and to have the Assistance of Counsel for his defence.

ARTICLE [VII]

In Suits at comon law, where the value in controversy shall exceed twenty dollars, the right of trial by jury shall be preserved, and no fact tried by a jury, shall be otherwise re-examined in any Court of the United States, than according to the rules of the common law.

ARTICLE [VIII]

Excessive bail shall not be required, nor excessive fines imposed, nor cruel and unusual punishments inflicted.

ARTICLE [IX]

The enumeration in the Constitution, of certain rights, shall not be construed to deny or disparage others retained by the people.

ARTICLE [X]

The powers not delegated to the United States by the Constitution, nor prohibited by it to the States, are reserved to the

States respectively, or to the people. [*First ten amendments declared in force December 15, 1791.*]

The Judicial power of the United States shall not be construed to extend to any suit in law or equity, commenced or prosecuted against one of the United States by Citizens of another State, or by Citizens or Subjects of any Foreign State. [*Declared in force January 8, 1798.*]

The Electors shall meet in their respective states, and vote by ballot for President and Vice-President, one of whom, at least, shall not be an inhabitant of the same state with themselves; they shall name in their ballots the person voted for as President, and in distinct ballots the person voted for as Vice-President, and they shall make distinct lists of all persons voted for as President, and of all persons voted for as Vice-President, and of the number of votes for each, which lists they shall sign and certify, and transmit sealed to the seat of the government of the United States, directed to the President of the Senate;—The President of the Senate shall, in the presence of the Senate and House of Representatives, open all the certificates and the votes shall then be counted;—The person having the greatest number of votes for President, shall be the President, if such number be a majority of the whole number of Electors appointed; and if no person have such majority, then from the persons having the highest numbers not exceeding three on the list of those voted for as President, the House of Representatives shall choose immediately, by ballot, the President. But in choosing the President, the votes shall be taken by states, the representation from each state having one vote; a quorum for this purpose shall consist of a member or members from two-thirds of the states, and a majority of all the states shall be necessary to a choice. * [And if the House of Representatives shall not choose a President whenever the right of choice shall devolve upon them, before the fourth day of March next following, then the Vice-President shall act as President, as in the case of the death or other constitutional disability of the President.]—The person having the greatest number

---

* The part enclosed by brackets has been superseded by section 3 of Amendment XX.

of votes as Vice-President, shall be the Vice-President, if such number be a majority of the whole number of Electors appointed, and if no person have a majority, then from the two highest numbers on the list, the Senate shall choose the Vice-President; a quorum for the purpose shall consist of two-thirds of the whole number of Senators, and a majority of the whole number shall be necessary to a choice. But no person consitutionally ineligible to the office of President shall be eligible to that of Vice-President of the United States. [*Declared in force September 25, 1804.*]

ARTICLE [XIII]

Section 1. Neither slavery nor involuntary servitude, except as a punishment for crime whereof the party shall have been duly convicted, shall exist within the United States, or any place subject to their jurisdiction.

Section 2. Congress shall have power to enforce this article by appropriate legislation. [*Declared in force December 18, 1865.*]

ARTICLE [XIV]

Section 1. All persons born or naturalized in the United States, and subject to the jurisdiction thereof, are citizens of the United States and of the State wherein they reside. No state shall make or enforce any law which shall abridge the privileges or immunities of citizens of the United States; nor shall any State deprive any person of life, liberty, or property, without due process of law; nor deny to any person within its jurisdiction the equal protection of the laws.

Section 2. Representatives shall be apportioned among the several States according to their respective numbers, counting the whole number of persons in each State, excluding Indians not taxed. But when the right to vote at any election for the choice of electors for President and Vice President of the United States, Representatives in Congress, the Executive and Judicial officers of a State, or the members of the Legislature thereof, is denied to any of the male inhabitants of such State, being twenty-one years of age, and citizens of the United States, or in any way abridged, except for participation in rebellion, or other crime, the basis of representation therein shall be reduced in the proportion which the number of such male citizens shall bear to the whole number of male citizens twenty-one years of age in such State.

Section 3. No person shall be a Senator or Representative in Congress, or elector of President and Vice President, or hold any office, civil or military, under the United States, or under any State, who, having previously taken an oath, as a member of Congress, or as an officer of the United States, or as a member of any State legislature, or as an executive or judicial officer of any State, to support the Constitution of the United States, shall have engaged in insurrection or rebellion against the same, or given aid or comfort to the enemies thereof. But Congress may by a vote of two-thirds of each House, remove such disability.

Section 4. The validity of the public debt of the United States, authorized by law, including debts incurred for payment of pensions and bounties for services in suppressing insurrection or rebellion, shall not be questioned. But neither the United States nor any State shall assume or pay any debt or obligation incurred in aid of insurrection or rebellion against the United States, or any claim for the loss or emancipation of any slave; but all such debts, obligations and claims shall be held illegal and void.

Section 5. The Congress shall have power to enforce, by appropriate legislation, the provisions of this article. [*Declared in force July 28, 1868.*]

ARTICLE [XV]

Section 1. The right of citizens of the United States to vote shall not be denied or abridged by the United States or by any State on account of race, color, or previous condition of servitude.

Section 2. The Congress shall have power to enforce this article by appropriate legislation. [*Declared in force March 30, 1870.*]

ARTICLE [XVI]

The Congress shall have power to lay and collect taxes on incomes, from whatever source derived, without apportionment among the several States, and without regard to any census or enumeration. [*Declared in force February 25, 1913.*]

ARTICLE [XVII]

The Senate of the United States shall be composed of two Senators from each State, elected by the people thereof, for six years; and each Senator shall have one vote. The electors in each State shall have the qualifications requisite for electors of the most numerous branch of the State legislatures.

When vacancies happen in the representation of any State in the Senate, the executive authority of such State shall issue writs of election to fill such vacancies: *Provided*, That the legislature of any State may empower the executive thereof to make temporary appointments until the people fill the vacancies by election as the legislature may direct.

This amendment shall not be so construed as to affect the election or term of any Senator chosen before it becomes valid as part of the Constitution. [*Declared in force May 31, 1913.*]

ARTICLE [XVIII]

[Section 1. After one year from the ratification of this article the manufacture, sale, or transportation of intoxicating liquors within, the importation thereof into, or the exportation thereof from the United States and all territory subject to the jurisdiction thereof for beverage purposes is hereby prohibited.

[Sec. 2. The Congress and the several States shall have concurrent power to enforce this article by appropriate legislation.

[Sec. 3. This article shall be inoperative unless it shall have been ratified as an amendment to the Constitution by the legislatures of the several States, as provided in the Constitution, within seven years from the date of the submission hereof to the States by the Congress.] [*Declared in force January 29, 1919 and repealed by Article xxi*].

ARTICLE [XIX]

The right of citizens of the United States to vote shall not be denied or abridged by the United States or by any State on account of sex.

Congress shall have power to enforce this article by appropriate legislation. [*Declared in force August 26, 1920.*]

ARTICLE [XX]

Section 1. The terms of the President and Vice President shall end at noon on the 20th day of January, and the terms of Senators and Representatives at noon on the 3d day of January, of the years in which such terms would have ended if this article had not been ratified; and the terms of their successors shall then begin.

Sec. 2. The Congress shall assemble at least once in every year, and such meeting shall begin at noon on the 3d day of January, unless they shall by law appoint a different day.

Sec. 3. If, at the time fixed for the beginning of the term of the President, the President elect shall have died, the Vice President elect shall become President. If a President shall not have been chosen before the time fixed for the beginning of his term, or if the President elect shall have failed to qualify, then the Vice President elect shall act as President until a President shall have qualified; and the Congress may by law provide for the case wherein neither a President elect nor a Vice President elect shall have qualified, declaring who shall then act as President, or the manner in which one who is to act shall be selected, and such person shall act accordingly until a President or Vice President shall have qualified.

Sec. 4. The Congress may by law provide for the case of the death of any of the persons from whom the House of Representatives may choose a President whenever the right of choice shall have devolved upon them, and for the case of the death of any of the persons from whom the Senate may choose a Vice President whenever the right of choice shall have devolved upon them.

Sec. 5. Sections 1 and 2 shall take effect on the 15th day of October following the ratification of this artcle.

Sec. 6. This article shall be inoperative unless it shall have been ratified as an amendment to the Constitution by the legislatures of three-fourths of the several States within seven years from the date of its submission. [*Declared in force February 6, 1933.*]

ARTICLE [XXI]

Section 1. The eighteenth article of amendment to the Constitution of the United States is hereby repealed.

Sec. 2. The transportation or importation into any State, Territory, or possession of the United States for delivery or use therein of intoxicating liquors, in violation of the laws thereof, is hereby prohibited.

Sec. 3. This article shall be inoperative unless it shall have been ratified as an amendment to the Constitution by conventions in the several States, as provided in the Constitution, within seven years from the date of the submission hereof to the States by the Congress. [*Declared in force December 5, 1933.*]

Section 1. No person shall be elected to the office of the President more than twice, and no person who has held the office of President, or acted as President, for more than two years of a term to which some other person was elected President shall be elected to the office of the President more than once. But this Article shall not apply to any person holding the office of President when this Article was proposed by the Congress, and shall not prevent any person who may be holding the office of President, or acting as President, during the term within which this Article becomes operative from holding the office of President or acting as President during the remainder of such term.

Sec. 2. This article shall be inoperative unless it shall have been ratified as an amendment to the Constitution by the legislatures of three-fourths of the several States within seven years from the date of it submission to the States by the Congress. [*Declared in force February 27, 1951.*]

Section 1. The District constituting the seat of Government of the United States shall appoint in such manner as the Congress may direct:

A number of electors of President and Vice President equal to the whole number of Senators and Representatives in Congress to which the District would be entitled if it were a State, but in no event more than the least populous State; they shall be in addition to those appointed by the States, but they shall be considered, for the purposes of the election of President and Vice President, to be electors appointed by a State; and they shall meet in the District and perform such duties as provided by the twelfth article of amendment.

Section 2. The Congress shall have power to enforce this article by appropriate legislation. [*Declared in force April 3, 1961.*]

Section 1. The right of citizens of the United States to vote in any primary or other election for President or Vice President, for electors for President or Vice President, or for Senator or Representative in Congress, shall not be denied or abridged by the United

States or any State by reason of failure to pay any poll tax or other tax.

Section 2. The Congress shall have power to enforce this article by appropriate legislation. [*Declared in force February 4, 1964.*]

Section 1. In case of the removal of the President from office or of his death or resignation, the Vice President shall become President.

Sec. 2. Whenever there is a vacancy in the office of the Vice President, the President shall nominate a Vice President who shall take office upon confirmation by a majority vote of both Houses of Congress.

Sec. 3. Whenever the President transmits to the President pro tempore of the Senate and the Speaker of the House of Representatives his written declaration that he is unable to discharge the powers and duties of his office, and until he transmits to them a written declaration to the contrary, such powers and duties shall be discharged by the Vice President as Acting President.

Sec. 4. Whenever the Vice President and a majority of either the principal officers of the executive departments or of such other body as Congress may by law provide, transmit to the President pro tempore of the Senate and the Speaker of the House of Representatives their written declaration that the President is unable to discharge the powers and duties of his office, the Vice President shall immediately assume the powers and duties of the office as Acting President.

Thereafter, when the President transmits to the President pro tempore of the Senate and the Speaker of the House of Representatives his written declaration that no inabilty exists, he shall resume the powers and duties of his office unless the Vice President and a majority of either the principal officers of the executive department or of such other body as Congress may by law provide, transmit within four days to the President pro tempore of the Senate and the Speaker of the House of Representatives their written declaration that the President is unable to discharge the powers and duties of his office. Thereupon Congress shall decide the issue, assembling within forty-eight hours for that purpose if not in session. If the Congress, within twenty-one days after receipt of the latter written declaration, or, if Congress is not in session, within twenty-one days after Congress is required to assemble, determines by two-thirds vote of both Houses that the President is unable to discharge the powers and duties of his office, the Vice President shall continue to discharge the same as Acting President; otherwise, the President shall resume the powers and duties of his office. [*Declared in force February 23, 1967.*]

BIBLIOGRAPHY

Beard, Charles A., *An Economic Interpretation of the Constitution of the United States* (Macmillan, 1964).

Commager, Henry Steele, *Great Constiitution* (Bobbs-Merrill, 1961), grades 6-10.

Dilliard, Irving, *Building the Constitution* (*St. Louis Post Dispatch*, 1961).

Farrand, Max, *The Framing of the Constitution of the United States*, Yale University Press, 1963).

Hamilton, A., Jay, J., and Madison, J., *The Federalist* (Modern Library, 1937).

Hammond, Harold E., Ed., *"We Hold These Truths"* (Cambridge Book Co., 1964).

McDonald, Forest, *We the People: The Economic Origins of the Constitution* (University of Chicago Press, 1958).

McGee, Dorothy Horton, *Framers of the Constitution* (Dodd, Mead, 1968).

Madison, James, *Notes of Debates in the Federal Convention of 1787* (Ohio University Press, 1966).

Miller, Loren, *The Petitioners* (Pantheon, 1966).

Morison, Samuel Eliot, *The Oxford History of the American People* (Oxford University Press, 1965).

Padover, Saul K., *The Living U.S. Constitution* (Mentor, The New American Library, 1963). Specifically pages 37–51, Major Pierce's Character Sketches.

Rossiter, Clinton, *1787: The Grand Convention* (Macmillan, 1966).

INDEX

Adams, John, 18
Adams, Samuel, 18
Amendments, Constitutional, provision for, 115-118
Anti-Federalists, 125, 126, 127, 134
Army, 93, 97
Articles of Confederation, 4, 12, 17, 18, 19, 20, 24, 25, 27, 29, 44, 45, 56, 57, 67-68, 75, 89-90, 97, 103, 109, 116, 134, 138, 140, 142, 143, 144, 145

Baldwin, Abraham, 55, 99, 149
Bassett, Richard, 143
Bedford, Gunning, Jr., 143
Bill of Rights, 121-122, 125, 126, 129, 133-135, 138, 146
Blair, John, 145
Blount, William, 147
Brearley, David, 51, 99, 140-141
Broom, Jacob, 144
Butler, Pierce, 18-20, 32, 59-60, 61, 80, 94, 99, 110, 148

Carroll, Daniel, 56-57, 78, 90, 99, 133, 144
Clinton, George, 16
Clymer, George, 141
Commerce, 4, 60, 113
Committee of Detail, 81-83, 87, 88-95, 96, 97, 99, 101, 102, 108, 113, 115, 119, 138, 139, 143, 149

Committee of the Whole, 23, 29-30, 42, 43, 48, 49, 50, 51, 53, 54, 55, 81, 82, 96, 138
Committee on Postponed Matters, 99-100, 137, 138, 141, 148
Committee on Style and Arrangement, 120, 139, 142
Common Sense (Paine), 18
Confederation, *see also* Articles of Confederation, 15, 16, 27, 45, 46, 48, 56, 68, 74, 75, 76, 82, 84-87
Connecticut, 21, 32, 48, 53, 63, 66, 70, 118, 126, 135, 139-140
Connecticut Compromise, 53-55, 82, 139
Constitution, U.S. (text), 151-174
Courts, state, 104
Currency, 17, 92

Daniel of Saint Thomas Jenifer, 144-145
Davie, William Richardson, 62, 78, 147
Dayton, Jonathan, 50-51, 67, 141
Declaration of Independence, 4, 10, 18, 19, 24, 43, 62, 85, 86, 91, 95, 122, 138, 140, 141, 142, 143, 147
Delaware, 12, 27-29, 30, 32, 43, 44, 48, 61, 63, 66, 68, 69, 70, 75, 113, 117, 126, 129, 143-144
Democracy, 16, 24-25, 31